Hellenic Studies 91

Greek Media Discourse
from Reconstitution of Democracy
to Memorandums of Understanding

Recent Titles in the Hellenic Studies Series

http://chs.harvard.edu/chs/publications

Greek Media Discourse from Reconstitution of Democracy to Memorandums of Understanding

TRANSFORMATIONS AND SYMBOLISMS

by

Nikoletta Tsitsanoudis-Mallidis

CENTER FOR HELLENIC STUDIES
Trustees for Harvard University
Washington, DC
Distributed by Harvard University Press
Cambridge, Massachusetts, and London, England
2022

*Greek Media Discourse from Reconstitution of Democracy to Memorandums of
 Understanding: Transformations and Symbolisms*
   By Nikoletta Tsitsanoudis-Mallidis
Copyright © 2022 Center for Hellenic Studies, Trustees for Harvard University
All Rights Reserved.
Published by Center for Hellenic Studies, Trustees for Harvard University,
   Washington, D.C.
Distributed by Harvard University Press, Cambridge, Massachusetts
   and London, England
Printed by Gasch Printing, Odenton, MD
Cover Design: Joni Godlove
Production: Kristin Murphy Romano

ISBN: 978-0-674-27258-3

Library of Congress Control Number (LCCN): 2022937715

Contents

Contents

PART III: The (Post-)Memorandum Language

PART IV: Reinforcing the Educational Role of the Media: A Modern Imperative

Preface

WHEN I DECIDED fifteen years ago to change my career path and leave the exciting job I had as a journalist, I could not imagine the powerful emotions that I would feel in the academic community. I was navigating in uncharted territory, unaware of the potential dangers, something that contributed to my subsequent career.

The great satisfaction I felt from transitioning to academia during the following years justified a relatively belated but deeply conscious choice to move from one demanding field to another, from the media into scientific research and teaching.

Given the amazing privilege of serving two seemingly different worlds, I faced what I considered to be a major challenge: attempting to connect them in the most systematic way possible. Like a poet talking about the poet as a symptom, I was called not only to analyze media discourse using the tools and principles of applied linguistics but to also construct bridges that would utilize the resounding power of media channels to the benefit of education.

The book you have in your hands is a product of this effort. It assembles my doctoral dissertation together with a new take on the rather subdued public discussion on the educational traits of the media—a discussion that should, in my opinion, be intensified by those who shape the public sphere. My skepticism is strong but devoid of the urge to outright reject the media which, as I argue, have the ability to respond appropriately when supported by academic discourse. Therefore, it is our responsibility to play the role of communicators and engage with the media in inventive ways. Even if some of these attempts fail, they will keep affecting the outcome.

My frame of reference is the reader that belongs to a new generation, a generation that ascribes no presumption of innocence to any kind of public discourse. These are the readers I seek, the active agents and players of communication. Every dismantlement, every deconstruction, is deliberate; it is an undertaking against the sovereignty of silence that has historically taken the side of authoritative and hegemonic discourse.

I will conclude this brief summary of thoughts by thanking the person who is a believer in and an exceptional guide of my work, the gifted Gregory Nagy, Francis Jones Professor of Classical Greek Literature and Professor of Comparative Literature, former Director of the Center for Hellenic Studies at Harvard University as well as his wonderful colleagues, Christos Giannopoulos, Managing Director at the Center for Hellenic Studies (Greece) at Harvard University, and Zoie Lafis, Managing Director at the Center for Hellenic Studies (USA) at Harvard University. I also want to offer my deep thanks to Nicolas Prevelakis, Lecturer in Social Studies at Harvard University and Assistant Director of Curricular Development at the Center for Hellenic Studies (USA) at Harvard University, for his encouragement and true support. I also want to deeply thank Leonard Muellner, Professor Emeritus of Classical Studies at Brandeis University, who also cooperates closely with the Center for Hellenic Studies (USA) at Harvard University on publishing and information technology issues. Additionally, I am grateful to the young fellow researchers Lefteris Kefalas and Marina Cheilitsi, for their great help and support and to Jill Curry Robbins, Production Manager for Publications at the Center for Hellenic Studies, and the copyeditor, Elizabeth Kresse, for meticulously editing the texts and the bibliography.

I would like to thank from the bottom of my heart Gutenberg Publications, Georgios and Costas Dardanos, as well as their staff who have supported my writing and research efforts, sharing with me a personal vision in times that have been proven conservative for, if not prohibitive of, any visionary journey.

Nikoletta Tsitsanoudis-Mallidis
Ioannina, February 2021

Foreword

Gregory Nagy

IT WAS in Nafplio, summer of 2013, where I first saw and heard Nikoletta Tsitsanoudis-Mallidis in action. She was giving a lecture in a seminar organized by Harvard University's Center for Hellenic Studies, and I was attending as a participant in that seminar. Still today, I recall so clearly how I marveled at her dynamism as a thinker and as a communicator. Already then, she was working on the essentials of the genial book for which I am writing this foreword. And, now that I am reading the book that stems from her prodigious research over the years, I marvel again at her dynamic brilliance: we see here a seasoned linguist who dares to confront the soul-crushing global crises experienced by humanity over the last few decades.

On the surface, this book by Professor Nikoletta Tsitsanoudis-Mallidis focuses on her native Greece, and how her native Greek language has evolved within the timeframe of a specific historical period, starting with the restoration of democracy in 1974 and proceeding through the economic crises signaled by a series of memoranda. The first such "memorandum of understanding" or MoU, made public in May 2010, recorded an agreement between the Greek Government on one side and, on the other side, the International Monetary Fund together with the European Union. This MoU, and the other memoranda that followed in its wake, is the critical moment of the "story" that takes shape in the form of the author's argumentation in her specialized role as a sociolinguist.

But the mental camera of our sociolinguist not only zooms in on the Greek language as it evolved in the historical context of the current Greek social crisis, with stunningly insightful analysis of the role of journalism and of media in general—including that ultimate opiate that is television. No, the "camera" of this stellar linguist also zooms out, viewing globally the relevance of the Greek crisis—soul-crushing in its own way—to the universal crises facing all humanity.

Confronting the crises that we all face in today's Iron Age, this inventive book by Nikoletta Tsitsanoudis-Mallidis gives me reason to hope, despite all the dangers endured nowadays by those who speak to power by analyzing the power of language. I find in the linguistic analysis of this author the foundations of the kind of humanism that will, I confidently predict, come to the timely rescue of humanity. That kind of humanism is alive and well in the Greek language, which ever sustains—whether consciously or unconsciously—the ideals of democracy.

Gregory Nagy
Francis Jones Professor of Classical Greek Literature and
Professor of Comparative Literature and Linguistics,
Harvard University

Director, Center for Hellenic Studies
Boston, October 24, 2019

Introduction

THIS BOOK constitutes an attempt to highlight the transformations in the forms and symbolic structures of media discourse in Greece that can be associated with its vernacularization during the period from the reestablishment of democracy in 1974 to the present day. I recorded the transformations that occurred in the discourse of media and journalism alongside the changes in views that accompanied those transformations by participating with a skeptical attitude in an open public dialogue on the power of discourse—not only as far as the description of *communicative events* is concerned but also in relation to its impact as a mode of social practice. This social practice, more often than not, constrains the ability of human subjects and of public discourse recipients to push back at the pressure exercised by those in authority, even when this pressure clearly stems from profit-driven motives and aims at exerting control. Detecting the limits of endurance in the face of those oppressive practices and of the consumption of explicit and implicit messages is an essential task, especially due to the ability of those in power to control and predetermine the dominant forms of discourse. Such control requires, on the one hand, the massification of society and, on the other hand, the passive acceptance by the readers of the view that power is exercised only in a top-down fashion and never in a bottom-up or dialectical way.

The book is divided into five chapters, and the first one commences, according to the conventions of academic protocol, with the theoretical approach of the functions of media discourse, emphasizing the authoritative function which is central to the rationale and the arguments developed throughout the whole of this book.

The second chapter consists of a review of the linguistic phenomena that have characterized Greek society and politics since the reestablishment of democracy. One of the main signposts of the transition to democracy in 1974 in Greece was the need to cultivate a new social and political culture.[1] Following these transformations, not only politicians but also actors of modern media

---

[1]   The linguistic and educational reform of 1976 is included in this context. The *language question* was resolved institutionally with the deletion of the language clause in 1987 which had been added to the 1974 Constitution by the dictatorship as well as with various laws that went into

adopted the vernacular language which acquired democratic connotations. The establishment of vernacular usage[2] was systematically favored as a development resulting from the reestablishment of democracy. The public suspicion that was associated with the vernacular character of spoken language retreated, and the end of formal style in public discourse occurred shortly after. The hyperbolic romanticism of archaic language transformed into an equally romantic usage of vernacular language as proof on the part of the political and media establishment of their sincere interest in the well-being of the *people*.[3] Media discourse followed the linguistic ideology of demoticism and, at the same time, the "authoritative" ideology of standard modern Greek language. The linguistic repertoire of journalists incorporated many of the elements of vernacular language from 1974 onward. Language was influenced while, at the same time, exercising influence on the language used by politicians. Their language, although remaining as authoritative as before as far as its content was concerned, inherited through the adoption of the vernacular connotations of progressive views and a common-people attitude (Fragkoudaki 1999:209). The introduction of free radio-television in the early 1990s encouraged the agents of electronic journalism to present themselves as familiar as possible to the recipients of their messages by assimilating their linguistic repertoire to that of their audience in the framework of what has been termed *communicative accommodation* (Coupland and Gilles 1988). Although journalists were prototypically vehicles of a highly-esteemed formal style, they abandoned the formality and strictness of the past and adopted an informal everyday-language characteristic of the common people. Modern "demoticists" originating from the politico-publishing establishment approached the "low" socio-economic strata through the laicity of their linguistic code and through the reintroduction of dialectal elements within the framework of a stance, which I termed stance of *highly fictive sympathy* or *illusive intimacy*.

---

effect during the K. Karamanlis administration in 1976 and the A. Papandreou administration in 1982.

[2] The demotic language is defined as the form of the Greek language that has been in use in oral speech by the Greeks for the past one hundred and fifty years and which was also shaped by literature. It is the popular language as opposed to the scholarly language, e.g. "I write/talk in demotic language." The ancient Greek adjective δημοτικός (popular/folk) is used to refer to many people based on the ancient phrase δημοτικά γράμματα (demotic letters), for example, "vernacular writing as opposed to holy letters, hieroglyphics." For more details, see *Dictionary of Standard Modern Greek* (2001:348). Correspondingly, the vernacular is defined as the language that belongs to, refers to, and addresses the people, originates in the people, expresses the people, or is created by the people. In other words, it is the language intended for the people; see *Dictionary of Standard Modern Greek* (2001:776).

[3] The concept is used here with its romantic allusions.

The entanglement of the language question with severe political conflicts resulted in the misplaced adoption of particular linguistic codes by particular political camps. The vernacular language was considered to be an exclusive tool of "progressive" political powers, while *katharevousa* (i.e. the archaic language) was associated with the "conservatives." Essentially, these pairings constitute a distorted projection of ideology on language.

In the following years, history repeated itself and the linguistic conflicts on the symbolic level did not cease. The recent and current political developments in Greece, such as the economic crisis and the various movements that developed, restored the symbolic natural habitat of the spoken vernacular, which is a habitat of political subversion and defiance against all kinds of authority. The symbolic load of vernacular language was charged with a revolutionary attitude; it was, however, associated with the efforts of the establishment to convince the masses of its social sensitivity as well. On the other hand, the wide usage of vernacular language during the recent development of the Greek version of the indignados movement cements the view that Greek vernacular language remains a diachronic and undisputed emblem of a subversive attitude, anti-establishment intentions, and of giving prominence to the true interests of the people.[4]

An interesting inversion was attempted immediately after when domestic and foreign politico-broadcasting systems employed the vernacular, not in order to defend the expectations and hopes of the people but in order to stigmatize the people as responsible for the country's entrance into the regime of MoUs[5] and financial supervision. Although the symbolization of language remained strong, it nevertheless changed domains, given that crucial ideological and cultural principles were transported to different hearths of power and wealth. Essentially, the symbolisms associated with vernacular language were rescued thanks to their alterations that took place through their enrichment with new dimensions.

The third chapter of the book contains the author's engagement with (post)memorandum language or "neo-language," which has vivid surprises in store for the researcher as far as the symbolic structures and the meanings of vernacular language usage are concerned. Although before the establishment

---

[4] For arguments against the street movements and media discourse in Greece during the crisis, see also Goutsos 2017.

[5] The first memorandum of understanding was signed by the Greek government, the International Monetary Fund, and the European Union in May 2010. It was an extensive agreement that describes the conditions under which Greece can receive regular loan installments from an agreed total sum of 110 billion euros in order to make payments toward previous loans. The agreement also includes measures to be taken by the government related to cutting salaries and pensions and the introduction of new taxes that will raise money for the administration.

of MoUs the vernacular was used by journalists, politicians and advertisers for the expansion of their audience and the formation of public opinion, after the imposition of the MoUs the same form of language was used in order to facilitate the manufacture of consent and the acceptance of harsh MoU measures. If the vernacular served a stance of fictive sympathy and illusive intimacy during the era of prosperity, the same language was employed in the era of MoU in order to stigmatize the people in general and each and every person separately for the economic dead-end in which Greece found itself. The emphasis laid on dramatized, plethoric, and manipulative public discourses is attributed to the attempt to manufacture consent and acceptance among the masses through the evocation of fear. Since the construction of fear requires incrimination, the economic crisis evolved to an embodied entity with clear fear-evoking properties and was then attributed to the "irresponsibility" of the low and middle socio-economic strata.

The conclusions of the third chapter of the book concern language usage in post-memorandum texts of the public sphere which have been published or posted in traditional and modern or alternative media (print media, electronic media, internet). The various discourse fragments were analyzed based on the principles of critical discourse analysis.

A new impressive element that emerges as a call for thought concerns a tendency for a "semantic revisionism," according to which words and phrases have acquired new meanings since the imposition of the MoUs. This process, which can metaphorically be described as a "re-christening" of words and phrases which acquire new meanings after repeatedly being dipped into the Jordan River of the memorandum discourse, this arbitrary and nomadic use of signifiers in order to depict different actions and situations, leads to a confusion on the part of the recipients, which in turn endangers the unanimity intended by certain media. It concerns a reformulation of meanings and ideas which are however depicted by the same old sound sequences, the same old acoustic images.[6]

While first-year undergraduate students in the introductory linguistics course are taught that changes in a linguistic sign necessitate the active consent of the respective speech community, consent which is by the way a factor of conservation; however, what really happened was violent transformations in the meanings and contents of words, without these transformations occurring through an unforced usage among the language users but through a top-down

---

[6] See also Tsitsanoudis-Mallidis 2011 in Section A of the Bibliography.

process of imposition and legitimation.[7] This phenomenon is not a Greek peculiarity but rather an international phenomenon.[8] It is an issue that is worth investigating and studying in the immediate future, and it is for now placed only on the periphery of this book.

The fourth chapter of this book is devoted to the need for enhancement of the educational role of the media as a strong antidote to the acknowledged pathogeny. I contribute my own proposals for less dominant and manipulative texts. It is obvious that I adopt the need for cultivation of the critical skills necessary to encode and deconstruct media discourse without, however, drawing the limit there. The reason for engineering proposals beyond the development of critical ability stems from my belief that knowledge is only misfortune if it is not complemented by a conviction that change is possible and by the cultivation of the confidence necessary for individuals to believe in their ability to bring about positive changes to the world, building their way up from their microcosmos to the public sphere through the invention and support of collectivities. As an initiative developed within this rationale, I refer to the International Summer University on Greek Language, Culture and Mass Media that I have organized and directed and to the Mini Seminars on Language and Communication which were offered not only to crowded lecture halls in the University of Ioannina but also to journalists, starting with the public Hellenic Broadcasting Corporation (ERT). Finally, I assert the survival and reinforcement of a neglected function of discourse—its aesthetics, beauty, and harmony.

---

[7] "Once the words were strong as knives. A journalist used texts that had a beginning, a middle, and an end. You read it and you could remember it. Today it seems that words have lost their meaning; they have often become weapons of misinformation, of propaganda in the shape of consensus, which the media and the politicians want to make universal and impose it for their own purposes. The harsh measures were named 'reforms,' the terrifying layoffs were called 'restructuring' or 'streamlining' and so on. This misuse of words, concepts, and ideas leads to the loss of meaning of those that need to be said, as well as to the loss of whatever action or reaction to the things those who raise objections disagree with, who are usually the most vulnerable and wronged" (Denaxa 2019).

[8] "For example, earlier this year Macron called the Yellow Vests a 'hateful mob.' The use of the term *mob* to characterize a political and social movement intends to deconstruct and criminalize it. The mob is unthinking and, in the sphere of collective imagination, this term evokes madness and absurdity. What did Macron do? He called the protesters a mob in order to stigmatize and marginalize them in the eyes of public opinion, in an attempt to erase the movement and to unimpededly continue the implementation of his administration's platform. Another tactic consists in using mild expressions to avoid scaring those who are going to face consequences and causing violent reactions, thus reshaping reality with absolutely no reactions. Venezuela is a prime example, regardless of who one supports and why. When you are the head of the opposition and haven't been elected or anything and you're asking the army to stop Maduro, then that is called a *coup* not a *rebellion*, as we see today" (Denaxa 2019).

PART I

THEORETICAL APPROACH

1

The Functions of Media Discourse

1.1 Initial Approach

THE DESCRIPTION of the meaning of discourse matured into its current stage after interesting theories emerged in the second half of the nineteenth century. From Benveniste's position that discourse recreates reality (1966:25, 28) and Ducrot's stance that it generates subjectivity and is a central component of the identity of the members of a social group (1980:4), discourse evolved into a normative object that imposes specific forms onto people in their interactions, requiring or even inventing certain terms or social structures (Fragkoudaki 1999:16). In essence, discourse attempts (sometimes successfully) a symbolic transformation of reality and experience into concepts, reestablishing experience that it has previously deconstructed in order to reconstruct it later. Discourse never ceases to be a highly representational system characterized by its economy, effectiveness, and influence.

Media discourse is a distinct form of discourse whose terms are defined mainly by the type of communication being carried out but also by the factors that take part in it (transmitter, receiver, message form, medium). It is a public discourse, in the sense that it is interested in the significant aspects of society. It is informative, often ideologically charged, and coercive. Rarely literary or scientific, it is supposed to be exact, clear, and concise. The structure of a journalistic text is oriented towards its effective comprehension by the receiver (Chatzisavvidis 2000:33). Furthermore, professional media discourse is essentially polyphonic, both in the sense of intertextuality since the journalistic text is informed by other documents and in the sense of stratification, due to the redrafts and interventions that occur until it reaches its final version. A question raised here is if there is a discrete variety of registers that characterize the sum of journalistic language and if we can talk about a *journalese* which would be immediately recognized by the recipients of media (Politis 2001:115–118).

Various linguists, such as Jucker (1992), conclude that when characterizing journalistic language, we should exclude hybrid texts like essays and texts that are irrelevant to current affairs (e.g. scientific articles). They also state that the succinct denomination of *journalistic language* does not define a strictly specified set of styles that can be compared with other known varieties, such as legal or theological languages. This difference is due to the fact that the language of professional journalists is, by necessity, eclectic as it is dictated by each separate tradition, each of which is defined by the context of history and society. Consequently, the term *media language* is less about the style and more about the typology of the substance of the texts created by professional journalists, who are more interested in spreading and commenting on the news (Politis 2001). However, the rapid and constant changes in technology always create new research fields and questions about the nature, challenges, and shifting characteristics of media discourse—be it conventional or alternative and cooperative—as well as about the sociological analysis of its particular semiological characteristics during certain time periods.

As for its functions, media discourse primarily serves the function of *mediation* between reality—as it is understood by the producer of the journalistic text, at least—and the receiver. In essence, it is a mediation between the knowledge acquired by the transmitter and the ignorance or the interest of the recipient in knowing about one or more realities. Secondarily, it serves a formative socializing and educational function since it affects, along with education, the formation of a meaning of the language in its users, while at the same time *shaping* conscience and ideology and educating, directly or indirectly, the communicatees. It produces, promotes, and projects language models. It introduces linguistic innovations and neologisms and expresses its stance regarding language (Chatzisavvidis 2000:35–37), which it can effectively influence.

What is lacking is a long overdue, yet crucial, function that media discourse should serve. It is the shrunken and, until today, consistently neglected *feedback function*. The enactment of practices and actions that would allow for the reinforcement of the feedback function against an authoritative or generally regulatory or normative media discourse would turn mass media into agents of democratic social wealth with objective news coverage being the first benefit.

Media discourse has been studied through critical discourse analysis as a powerful field of projection, ideological roles, and confrontations with language being treated as an instrument of authority, control, and social formation of reality. Fairclough (1995) has warned about communication practices that are characterized by a lack of transparency, which results in the recipients of various texts not recognizing the ideologies served by these but also about the dangers stemming from their (automatic) reproduction.

After all, critical discourse analysis implies that the ideology of a text is often more implicit than it is, which is why it attempts to approach the issue differently through content analysis. It focuses on articulating the essence of texts as well as the social and political issues that are associated with them and their creation. The substance of language is always pre-prepared; in other words, it is organized and prepared by the dominant ideologies and the socio-political environment. Language form does not mechanically reflect reality but, to a large extent, creates reality itself and the knowledge we have of it (Georgakopoulou and Goutsos 1999:40–41, 218). In this context, every extensive linguistic or ideological-critical analysis of media discourse is extremely interesting in itself, which is why such analyses have been attempted systematically in Greek academic circles for the past two decades.

1.2 Aspects and Characteristics of Media Discourse

1.2.1 As social discourse

The observed language polymorphy and its social dimension are directly related to journalism to the extent that media discourse or the journalistic language ascribe and express information and experiences that (should) come from all social strata that have, in turn, their own language varieties (Politis 2001:115). Besides, the meaning that words acquire based on their social context and on the social relations of the speakers is more important than their literal meaning (Fragkoudaki 1999:37).[1] Furthermore, media discourse is characterized by its socializing function in the sense of the person's integration into society (Chatzisavvidis 2000:39) but also of the shaping of so-called public opinion. According to Chatzisavvidis, the journalists' discourse is an ideological product, which does not necessarily solely represent the ideology of the speaker but also results from the individual set of beliefs that people who shape the overall ideology have, drawing the (ideological) line of the medium through which media discourse is transmitted. That ideology, or at least some of its elements, is subsequently spread to various social groups. As a result, every study of media discourse requires a deep knowledge of its varieties as well as of the social and other aspects that media discourse is associated with.

It is in the interest of the media and of journalists to reveal the special elements of a multilevel and polymorphic social reality. Journalists are asked by the groups themselves to show interest in them, either by choosing appropriate topics to research and cover or by respecting the language codes and the ethnic identity of a specific language community (Tsokalidou 2001:115), without

---

[1] Besides the social context, the political and economic contexts are also crucial, as will be shown in the third chapter of this book.

racism or prejudice and away from stereotypical notions.[2] This is a necessary condition for media discourse—including the discourse transmitted through television—to be accepted by members of every language community who, as long as they feel that they are being treated tactfully and with respect by journalists and the media, develop a sense of trust and security toward the media.

When it is not confined by stereotypes and prejudices, media discourse today sometimes chooses to use language forms belonging to other languages, mainly English, which are supposed to add prestige and a vague communication glamour. It is also often characterized by arbitrariness and exaggeration in the context of an increasing tendency to adopt a conversational style (a process called *conversalization*).[3] One of the consequences of these choices is *factual distortion* (Valiouli 2001:9–26), which inflates the meaning of words leading to their complete annihilation (Diamantakou 2001) and to loss of credibility in the eyes of the recipients.

Media discourse also influences the language of its recipients, given the educational attributes[4] of a public discourse that is transmitted to a wide audience through popular and prestigious channels. As a result, the designers and institutions of media discourse are practically obligated to recognize and respect the language varieties of a community and to choose topics to research based on the representation of a plethora of social groups. Furthermore, it is imperative for community members to be able to intervene in how journalists choose their topics, which will have to cover both their problems and their interests. This intervention has to be true and not mediated or filtered because, otherwise, the medium will project its own views. Popular representation cannot be mobilized as a striking piece of evidence of a supposed democratic and honest approach of the medium to society.

1.2.2 As ideological discourse

Language not only expresses but also reproduces a hierarchical social reality. In addition, the representatives of various authorities misuse their social legitimacy as transmitters and turn language into a weapon that exerts violence. This is the basis of Fragkoudaki's standpoint when she introduces the term *ideological language*. She defines it as the misuse of legitimacy that produces acceptance, giving the language of authority magic traits, thus violating communication and silencing the receiver. She posits that ideological language nullifies the

---

[2] For example, the immigration issue and its depictions in the press, both Greek and international, was a strong crash test regarding the strength of these stereotypes. For more, see also Tsitsanoudis-Mallidis N. and E. Derveni 2018:1–38.

[3] On conversalization or orality, see Androutsopoulos 2001:167–183.

[4] On the educational function of media discourse, see also Chapter Four.

bidirectional attribute of discourse and that the receiver can no longer play the role of an equal participant in the conversation. It destroys the polarity of discourse and replaces it with an authoritative monologue that has a specific form which extorts the receiver and protects the transmitter from the logical processing of messages and, thus, from criticism. Ideological language, meaning "the use of a language that entraps and defrauds," produces acceptance of what the speaker says in an extortionate way. "Despite and beyond meaning, and sometimes despite the absence of meaning," it is a pluralistic, axiological, euphemistic, mixed, dichotomic, and self-evident *discourse*. It exerts violence on the receiver through misapprehension, unintelligibility, silencing, or repression of opposing discourses (Fragkoudaki 1999:154–155, 182).

Building upon this theory, I will now make a series of observations seeking to find the differences and the similarities in form between ideological language and media discourse. I will focus on discourse transmitted through television, which receives the most exposure.

1. Is media discourse pluralistic? Media discourse on television has a lot of pluralistic elements in its form, such as the high frequency of certain types, rhetorical repetition, vaunting, use of foreign idioms, neologisms, and systematic use of vernacularized structures. The latter, along with neologisms and clichés, can potentially serve the cultivation of fictive sympathy towards the receiver.[5] In other words, the journalist and the medium may appear approachable, understanding, and friendly to the receivers, whose interests they are supposed to be serving.

On the contrary, contemporary media discourse on television does not appear to have other elements that would characterize a discourse as pluralistic, such as the use of long periods, archaic and complex syntax, sophisticated syntactic structure, rare and refined words and phrases,[6] or the systematic use of ancient words. Avoiding such flamboyances is not owed to the need for speedy communication but to the necessity to limit vagueness, confusion, and verbose expressions. There are of course *ambiguities* and *semantic achromaticities* (Babiniotis 1994:196). As a general rule, the goal is clarity and fast transmission of easily understood concepts.

The existence of an ideological property, however, requires the exposition of a fact, either before or after, in a vocabulary that will signify something unprecedented, phenomenal, and unique. In this context, media discourse is a

---

[5]   This attitude will be thoroughly discussed in Chapter Two.

[6]   This description will be reversed, especially as far as Greece is concerned, from 2010 onwards when the country will enter the memoranda period. These changes in language will be discussed in Chapter Three.

reflection in a distorting mirror (Chatzisavvidis 2000:71). Fiske argues that, from a textual point of view, there are not huge differences between news broadcasts and TV shows (whether one-off or recurring episodes). "Television's love for dramatic presentations of stories that are based on real events shows how easy it is for its textual forms to surpass the wider limits between fact and fiction." And he adds: "In textual terms, the news may not be all that different from a soap opera" (2000:415).

The receivers then think that they communicate, understand, judge, and retain their role as one of the two main actors of communication. In essence, however, they are trapped inside a fake role in a fake attempt to communicate, exactly because of the violent destruction brought upon television's polarity by the "terrorizing" dominance of the transmitter, who maintains and solidifies the distance of his superiority as an expert. We inevitably arrive at the question of whether the pluralistic form can make the communicatees take responsibility for any possible gaps in their understanding of the message or even lead them to a kind of subjection of silence for fear that their inability to comprehend is an admission of their unworthiness. [7]

2. Is media discourse axiological? Media discourse is characterized by its axiological character and form. Inside the speaker's or journalist's vocabulary, sentence structure, grammar, and syntax there are hidden assessments and judgments of people and situations that extort the recipient to accept them so that the latter will not have any way to challenge not just the explicit but also the implicit messages that they receive. For example, words with significant moral weight—like *people, tradition, nation*—reinforce the transmitted message to the point that any further justification and proof of the claims included is rendered redundant. According to Fragkoudaki, (1999:162) there are words/values that create messages impervious to any change. However, the media often use other phrases, such as "informing public opinion," "objectivity," and "informing the citizen or in the service of information," which refer to and are supported by unalienable democratic rights or by unquestionable values and principles. These phrases are recruited and idolized. They serve the agents of public discourse, and their goal is to effectively form and control public opinion in a way that is convenient for the existing powers and that will keep them at the top of the social, political, or economic hierarchies. The communicatee is bound to not even think to challenge what is "self-evident," unless they are contrarian, prone to resistance, or simply eccentric.

---

[7] For more information, see the Bibliography, Section C for a link to my TED lecture on this topic.

3. Is media discourse mixed? Media discourse can sometimes create mixes of language and meaning that may impede understanding and critical examination of a message. If we consider that one of the goals is to create an attractive product, then it is easier to discern the reason why discourse can sometimes take and adopt abstract forms, even in its basic structures.

4. Euphemistic expressions are often used in media discourse, which give undoubted prestige to its agent and the medium itself, making the messages transmitted appear beyond reproach and criticism. Journalists and the media they work for proclaim that they are "objective," "unfettered," "independent," and "free," thus legitimizing, albeit arbitrarily, the function of the medium and its authorized information agent. Euphemistic expressions are included in implicit and explicit ways that reinforce the cultivation of a (pseudo)impression of objectivity[8] or independence of the medium. Media discourse attempts to appear objective, unfettered, and independent, without it being so and without it being possible to be so (Eco n.d.:34–38).[9]

5. Furthermore, in media discourse, just as in political discourse, *the subject that speaks is silenced or transferred from the "I" to the axiological "we"* (for example, "We provide objective news coverage to our viewers"), so this is automatically juxtaposed with "others" without their identity always being clarified and without any concrete proof about why "they" do not have the same capabilities that are implicitly contained in "us." This visible or concealed confrontation alludes to another characteristic of ideological discourse: dichotomy (Fragkoudaki:173). This confrontation between two given values exists beforehand, and each statement is based on the continuous, indirect, and implicit contrast between good and evil, moral and immoral, right and wrong, progressive and reactionary.[10] Journalists take the side of morality, truth, or justice from

---

[8] An experiment I often perform with my students in order for them to realize the difficulties and the fluidity of the concept of objectivity is this: during class I ask all of them to write fifty words in three minutes describing what happens and what they perceive. They are all witnesses of the same event in time and in place. Next, they are asked to read their texts to one another. Their depictions and descriptions differ, sometimes dramatically, which in turn sparks a discussion about the concept of objective description. In the second stage, I separate the class into two groups. The first group has to deconstruct the lesson and the teacher and the second to elevate and commend the process. In other words, I tell them to use a partial and axiologically weighted discourse. We then read what they have written, and we discuss the variety of the contents and the extremes these contents can go to when discourse is regulated by goals and intentions.

[9] See also: 1.2.3.1.

[10] For example, in the annual report of the European Commission against Racism and Intolerance (ECRI) for 2016, there is mention of "a political climate in which foreigners are portrayed as a threat to one's own identity, culture and economic prosperity" (see the Bibliography, Section C for a link to the report). Also, in September 2019, the decision made by the new president of

the very beginning and are called to face what's evil, unethical, wrong, or false, without having to justify why they're associated with these values since it is enough to bring them up in order to be connected and identified with them, at least fictitiously.[11] Just like politicians who use ideological language,[12] journalists represent public opinion by asking their guests various questions during their shows or through their interventions. They transcribe the emotions and the reactions of the public and generally act in its best interests (so they claim). In a way, it is an attempt for their discourse to become potent and irrefutable and thus to limit possible challenges to it.

6. It is self-evident that media discourse is axiological, assuring, euphemistic and, ultimately, an authoritative discourse that carries definitive messages that have been deemed true and unfalsifiable beforehand, even if they would normally need to be accompanied by proof. Phrases such as "reliable sources," "well-informed circles," and "according to confirmed information" are pools of legitimization and validity in which their discourse is consecrated as reliable, true, authentic, and prone to reason, knowledge, and common sense.

1.2.3 As authoritative discourse

The fact that critical discourse analysis focuses on journalistic discourse (Fairclough 1995) can be interpreted to the point where what is mostly promoted in—and is served through—said discourse is but the dominant ideological roles, goals, and intentions. For example, the lack of transparency, which facilitates the effectiveness of communication practices that hide

---

the Commission, Ursula von der Leyen, to rename the portfolio on immigration and security as the portfolio for "protecting the European way of life" was met with harsh criticism (see the Bibliography, Section C for a link to a newspaper article on this issue). See also Tsakiroglou 2019.

[11] The element of dichotomy has been discussed a lot in the public discourse of Greece for the past few years. The programs that the Hellenic Broadcasting Corporation (ERT) showed are indicative of that. See the Bibliography, Section C for a link to my 2017 workshop on journalistic language at the ERT Respect Words seminar on journalism and hate speech. Similar questions were addressed during the Fifth International Summer University on Greek Language, Culture and Media held from July 7 to July 14, 2019, with the topic "The Language of the 'Other': The Ethics of Otherness." See also 4.1.1 and 4.4 as well as the article "Syros and 'the Language of the Other'" (a link to the article is provided in the Bibliography, Section C).

[12] Georgakopoulou and Goutsos (1999:206) bring up a classical analysis that Fairclough (1989) conducted of a radio interview given in 1985 by Margaret Thatcher, then prime minister of the United Kingdom. In this analysis, he examines the use of pronouns and the ways Thatcher artfully used the pronoun "we," sometimes to talk about the British people in general, sometimes to refer to her party (the Tories), and sometimes even in a misleading way ("we the privileged"), as opposed to the pronoun "they" that served the creation and projection of groups of otherness. Her discourse was characterized by strong deontic modality as was shown by the use of verbs such as must, ought to, etc.

the government's real ideology from the communicatees, is one of the most important issues for sustained research and analysis. The unquestioning and uncontrollable acceptance of every transmitted message by receivers that lack critical skills or are media illiterate could be dangerous for themselves and the community in which they act and develop. Based on Chatzisavvidis's descriptions and analyses (2000:40), media discourse is an authoritative discourse, as it imposes silence and subjection on the receiver and is uttered by a person who is authorized by society as an agent of authority (such as a politician, a priest, an educator). It evokes truth and objectivity, is full of slogans, and its producer has access to sources of information and to the mechanisms that bring messages to the public.

The recording of the transmitter's power and superiority over the receiver deprives the latter of their right to intervene and, consequently, of their participation in an equal society, creating a state of passivity that can even be supported emotionally by the pleasure derived from "the signifiers of passivity" (Semoglou 2001:271–272). And when the subject—the individual—is massified through the mediation of his/her anxieties and expectations, then the initial reactions and responses can potentially be weakened or even disused.

Here, I would like to incorporate the concept of *lingual hegemony* (Christidis 2001:311), which refers to the mechanisms employed by the exercise of ideological power used to secure consent for the dominant class's choices by making them sound natural, leading to their easy acceptance. Some of the aspects of lingual hegemony, a concept that is associated with the Italian thinker Gramsci, include the rejection of dialects, the imposition of a single dialect as an official national language, the normalization of the linguistic variety of the language the upper classes use, the domination of the English language, and so on.[13] Furthermore, media discourse is coercive without necessarily being authoritarian because it is shaped in conditions that are similar to power discourse, while the means through which media discourse is transmitted have been self-proclaimed as a sector of truth.

I would like to suggest an additional characteristic that would confirm the authoritative character of media discourse. It is about the fact that it appears serious and substantial since it gives the impression that it is only interested in significant matters that are of public interest. These "significant" matters are characterized as such after they have been interpreted and assessed by the journalist/the media. They are all the more supported by stigmatizing and axiological adjectives.

---

[13] According to Van Dijk (1993:121–142), journalistic texts reproduce the relations between authority and political, social, and cultural hegemony by using a series of media due to which some social or ethnic groups become excluded or oppressed.

There is, however, a counterpoint: When private television was first established, media discourse started showing interest not only in public affairs but
also in issues that were of minor importance to public life.[14] This choice can be
associated with the offering of topics the receivers/consumers are familiar with
but also with the desire to disorient receivers by giving them pleasant topics.
Giving prominence to the personal stories or experiences of ordinary people
regarding events in the public sphere was not exclusive to reality shows but
infiltrated the very core of news broadcasts. The reasons for this change cannot
be exclusively ideological; they have to be commercial as well.

1.2.3.1 Relation to objectivity

While Eco posits that journalists' discourse is by default unable to be objective
(n.d.:34–38), according to Chatzisavvidis, the media claim to be objective in
order to cultivate and maintain the prestige of the mediation they perform. A
possible decrease in this prestige leads to the decline of the collective conscience
acquired by the individual through the information provided by the press. The
latter mentions the phenomenon of *pseudoobjectivity,* pointing out that there
are times when journalists prefer, even if they do not realize it at the time, a
pseudoobjectivity when there is a choice between objectivity and subjectivity
because they try to present facts that are devoid of any subjective judgment,
while ignoring that this is impossible (Chatzisavvidis 2000:28, 70).

In my opinion, the media serve two simultaneous functions, which can
be contradictory at times. On the one hand there is the informative function
and on the other the propaganda function or the function of manufacturing
consent. These two functions sometimes clash or even undermine each other.
The first function, which is purely informative, can give shape to the collective
conscience among recipients, while the second is interested in shaping opinions, attitudes, and ideologies, either by manufacturing consent or by preparing
the ground for subverting existing connections. Objective information—with all
the caveats that can accompany the adjective "objective"—give prestige to the
medium, so it can control and shape collective conscience. On the other hand,
the non-objective information provided by the media, which is associated with
an increased propagandistic function, brings about a reduction of prestige in
the medium and long runs. This results in a reduction of control capabilities—in
other words, a reduction in the ability to shape the collective conscience of the
individuals it addresses.

---

[14] For example, during the October 8, 2003, news broadcast at ALPHA, Nikos Chatzinikolaou, the
anchor, presented a story titled "Going to work with the Tupperware," which referred to the fact
that many workers and employees went to work with their lunch in a plastic bowl.

Variety and pluralism at the level of the media make them operate in the most objective way of transmitting information possible. When pluralism exists, the medium is relatively committed due to competition among the media, and the recipients are prone to comparison. Of course, the fact that there is a plethora of media today does not provide a safeguard against a propagandistic function given that many media belong to an individual or a specific closed dominant group. This results in a fraudulent form of pluralism and variety since the media are asked to serve the interests of the few and not of the many.

1.2.3.2 Authoritative/reductive and cooperative/additive relations

New elements can come up in the authoritative aspects of media discourse if we examine its relation to educational discourse within the classroom. I do not think this kind of comparison would be unfair for two reasons. Firstly, both discourses come from agents of authority legitimized by society, which makes them authoritative discourses; secondly, media discourse has an educational function. Media discourse possesses a function that shapes opinions but also educates, not only by shaping the language of its recipients but also by shaping their conscience and ideology, thus educating the recipients of its messages directly or indirectly.

Another essential characteristic of journalistic language pertains to its ability to negotiate the social identities of its recipients. Correspondingly, the social and lingual identities of students in a classroom are also a point of contention which leads, depending on the case, to their reinforcement or diminishment. Such perceptions can be associated with the uses of journalistic language in order to reach useful conclusions.

I will therefore start with the distinction between *authoritative/reductive relations* or *coercive relations of power* and *cooperative/additive relations* or *collaborative relations of power* (Cummins 2002:57–64), and I will apply these principles to the study of "routine" electronic journalism. Before that, however, I will try to define the concepts based on Cummins's arguments.

- *Authoritative relations* refer to the exercise of power by a dominant group (person or country) over a subordinate group, based on the axiom that the amount of power is stable and functions as a zero-sum game. The dominant group defines and subsequently legitimizes the subordinate group as inferior, subservient, or vicious, thus making itself superior. This process automatically leads to the emergence of limitations (social or psychological) in the inferior and unprivileged groups or people. In essence, authoritative relations function in a way that maintains the social structure of power—that is, the existing distribution of wealth and power. As for schools, the fact that students coming from lower social and economic strata fail in class is attributed to supposed inherent characteristics of the group itself, such as diglossia, parental indifference, or even genetic inferiority. As a result, authoritative relations function reductively and undermine the process of reinforcing the identities of the children, especially when the authoritative balance is closed and favors the official authorities, which are represented by the teacher and, by extension, the educational community.

- *Cooperative relations* do not view power as a stable and predefined quantity owned by certain groups but as a product of relations among persons and groups in the classroom, where students feel that their identity is accepted and that they are themselves capable of bringing about changes both in their own lives and in their social situation. This relation works additively; students are *strengthened* through cooperation with the teacher as power is created when all work together and is not imposed by others. Identities are not static and predefined but can be reshaped through experience and proper encouragement by the agents of teaching.

And now I will attempt to apply this theory to the mass media. The huge influence of the press on society, especially on language norms, information, opinion but also on a general way of life (consumerism and so on) leads to the conclusion that the mass media are a dominant form of authority that is exercised by a group of people (owners of TV or radio stations, newspapers, magazines, and other types of print media as well as top executives and journalists) on the masses. The dominant group (mass media) keeps for itself the role of the expert and considers itself "superior" to the masses/public, on which it believes it can impose its own worldview. This view, for example Lippmann's view on the news, has existed since the late 1970s and is characteristic of a certain point of view of the dominant group. "The news," he claims, "is not the mirror of social events, but the report given by those who impose their own point of view" (1979:3). To extend this crucial view, I would add that the news is what a closed and sealed hierarchy decides to present and ultimately to impose as "news" to serve its own goals.

The process of defining various groups or individuals as inferior, subordinate, and non-experts ends up in a type of interactive relations, which imposes limits on them (economic, psychological, social). For example, ordinary people do not have the right to acquire their fifteen minutes of fame, unless they have found themselves in the unfortunate position of being eyewitnesses to a horrible event (e.g. a traffic accident) or unless they behave in extreme ways which are mostly negative and rarely positive. In other words, citizens will have to become heroes or victims to enter the public eye. Even if the media believe that a citizen should take up some of that valuable TV or radio time, the duration and intervention are determined strictly by the media and not the citizen.

In this case, authoritative relations function in a way which maintains the distance between the media and the viewer and, ultimately, the distribution of power and wealth within the society. Such functions are connected to a wider environment of commercialization that characterizes informational and advertising products (Tsitsanoudis-Mallidis 2011).

Furthermore, the frequency with which the media-journalistic discourse is converted into media-advertising discourse and the bombardment of recipients with slogans and other stereotypical phrases can lead to a gradual desensitization of the public's sense of the language, especially among the people who are less resistant to the various appealing television fads. Images have turned into gods, leading to a primitive state in which visual representations dominate over descriptions and analyses of situations.

The existence and persistence of such an authoritative relation between the media and the public is also manifested in the interest some people outside the media have in acquiring their own media companies. According to Kyrtsos (2003:26), this model of the dynamic, up-and-coming capitalist had the following characteristics at the beginning of the 1980s: "a centrist or left-wing political profile collaborating with the socialist countries of the Eastern bloc, penetrating into the field of mass media in one way or another."

On the other hand, cooperative relations treat the concept of power not as a predetermined quantity but as a product of relations among persons and groups (Cummins 2002:58–60). In the case of electronic media, in order to promote and maintain a relation that reinforces the public that consumes these media, the recipients will have to feel that their identity (language codes, social origins, gender and so on) is accepted and that they have the ability to bring changes to their lives and their social situation by giving publicity to their problems. As long as this condition is met, then the relation between receiver and transmitter works additively and a collaborative creation of power gradually becomes a reality.

The study of the way media discourse is used to create so-called common sense which leads, in turn, to unanimity and consensus regarding initiatives and measures that serve the interests of particular groups is also interesting. Just like in the case of social discourse, media discourse—which belongs, after all, to social discourse—is often recruited by the dominant class or its representatives—especially when they have the privilege of owning media corporations—in order to function as a force that will make the recipients/subordinates internalize the fact that they are subjects of that power and, in the next stage, to make them passively accept it.

Language becomes an instrument of power, the vehicle that handles and changes power relations among people. The ways in which social discourse functions in order to "manufacture consent" (Chomsky 1987) can be described with the use of the Gramscian concept of *hegemony*, which states that consent is created through invisible cultural domination and not through visible political authority (Corson 1993:1, 6). This non-coercive power can penetrate into conscience itself, and the subordinates become accomplices in their own subjection. Thus, power hegemonies are reinforced and reproduced. The subordinates attach themselves to language norms that have been created by the dominant groups, without realizing that they are voluntarily forced to do so. On the other hand, journalists, who are the personification of the power of the media, can recognize the religion, ideology, and culture belonging to those who are culturally different as respectable and organized forms of self-expression and encourage their development. In such cases, they help and encourage the process of challenging and, consequently, gradually diminishing the dominant behaviors within a wider society but also the authoritative structures that cause and maintain these behaviors.

In conclusion, in the case of authoritative relations, the goal is for the recipients to react as little as possible or for their responses to become as predictable and manipulatable as possible. Another goal is for the communicator to be identified with the beginning of a communicative initiative, which begins and ends based on the communicator's intentions and expectations with as few unpredictable developments as possible, which is hard, or even impossible, for the communicator to control. On the contrary, in the case of cooperative/additive relations, the goal is for the communicatees/recipients themselves—in other words, the many—to be able, allowed, and encouraged to initiate communication, so the communicator is the one that has to enter the process of response which, in turn, will be the next stimulus for the continuation of communication.

It is true, however, that authoritative (by force) relations still have not been converted to cooperative and additive relations within a caring society in which the journey and the navigation of otherness and difference will not have predefined and predictable outcomes (Cummins 2002:280). As far as media discourse is concerned, there is now a pressing need to shape it anew and change it to a type of discourse that will not be controlled and dominated by a desire for absoluteness. It is not going to be presented as a deified product but as a creation guided by the relativity of power and the inability of mediation (Chatzisavvidis 2000:73). In such a case, media discourse could bravely consider its presence as a reflection in a distorted mirror which is, in turn, perceived as equally distorted by its recipients. And there is no doubt that this distorted image would cease to be considered identical to the real one.

1.2.3.3 Subjection of silence

How real is communication between mass media and their recipients? How effectively communicative can media discourse be given that its nature and medium necessarily involve presenting the discourse of *one* against the undefinable *many*? How can people who do not know one another communicate truly and effectively? How is communication even possible when one, the transmitter, does not know who the recipients are exactly and when they consume media and to what extent their attention is turned to the broadcast? To what degree and in what way do the recipients of an electronically transmitted media discourse retain their role as equal participants in the "conversation"?

If we accept the fact that communication loses its interactive components when the transmitter manages to impose silence on the receiver, then the communication between journalist and viewers/audience or even readers could a priori reduce expectations. Even if we believe that the receivers are coerced into silence in the face of invisible power, the peculiarities of the communication channel should be considered, as they impose a different view of the characteristics of communication, even when the latter is characterized as fraudulent or fictitious. In my opinion, the receivers of media discourse retain their role as equals to a great extent, no matter whether they react by presenting their own discourse against that of the journalist's, whether they refuse to claim responsibility for this fictitious communication, or whether they refuse to become recipients. The receivers are strengthened by these characteristics, as this kind of control is active and dynamic, causing stress and anxiety to journalists and other members of the media. One has to be aware of this kind of strength.

This way, the destruction of communication—in the sense that the transmitter appropriates and possibly misappropriates the exclusive right to monologue which silences the receiver—can be averted. However, complacency toward the all-powerful audience of television and radio cannot last. That's because audiences are by nature fragmented due to economic, social, and other factors.[15]

At the same time, various mechanisms and functions that have been prepared and designed within the media seem that they favor the media—or even appropriate the right of the public to public discourse.[16] This is an attempt

---

[15] See also section 1.2.3.4.

[16] For example, by hosting live interventions by the audience, by bringing citizens to various political shows, by broadcasting live from places where citizens are gathered and so on.

to make a so-called opening to society so it can, in turn, support and reward the medium and its agents/transmitters of media discourse with increased viewership and ratings, which is important for a media corporation—whether public or private—to succeed in a very competitive advertising market.

1.2.3.4 The "manifold" audience

The public can be considered a divided or manifold entity right from the start (Moschonas 1995:182–183). Its multilevel stratification is accompanied by many variables, such as age, gender, family status, education, profession etc. These variables are connected, in turn, to the shaping of the audience's opinion, which is called *public opinion*, or of other types of reaction. It is a pliable spiral of interconnections that are often complex and fluid.

There are many references to what the audiences consist of and how they influence the message in the fields of ethnography of communication[17] and of pragmatics, especially in discourse analysis. No matter how passive the audiences are and how little they lend themselves to theoretical analysis, the characteristics of the live audiences present in the studio during political shows vary, even when their composition is designed in advance. And that's because the social hierarchy is evident in these, and they can also serve some commercial interests. There are also cases when audiences are part of live shows and have a specific and limited role in each participation framework of a particular speech event.

Theory, however, has moved on from the static view of a passive receiver to the view of the receiver as an active co-creator of communication (Georgakopoulou and Goutsos 1999:210; Bakhtin 1981). This shift has been achieved mainly through the analysis of conversations, where the relationship between speaker and audience can be traced on the level of how to adjust speech based on the audience. In communication accommodation theory (Coupland and Giles 1988), the variable most studied is the age of the audience.

As far as journalists are concerned, media audiences are potential audiences, even though there is, at least in theory, the possibility of feedback in the form of personal interventions. This potentiality, as a characteristic of audiences, (over)defines the organization of virtual signs in every medium—content, style, and semiotics. However, the audience of communication media is nothing more than a fabrication of mass communication and the interests it serves. The counterpoint to its all-embracing power is the social, economic, and other stratification, the fragmentation of audiences that leads to an individualized

---

[17] See also Saville-Troike 1982:chap. 4.

viewing, listening, or reading of the messages transmitted by the media (Politis 2001:116).

Goffman (1981:131–144) believes that the term *audience* is multivalent and deserves deeper analysis, as it refers to concepts that correspond to different roles of the audience. There are at least four different roles: official addressed recipient, official unaddressed recipient, eavesdropper, and overhearer (Levinson 1988:165–174). The latter occurs when a member of the audience does not have a formal position in a speech event, as in the case of listening in on a telephone call (Moschonas 2005:183).

As far as television is concerned, I would argue that the role of the audience is twofold. The TV viewers are both eavesdroppers and legitimate receivers or recipients since the presence of discourse agents in television or elsewhere is judged by them to a certain extent. This presence is legitimized, not as in the case of the jurors in a courtroom but in a wider sense. On the other hand, the viewers of a TV show are *listeners*, without being directly talked to, as would happen if they had a physical presence in the conversation or were receivers of a live conversation. The agents of TV discourse, however, can randomly appeal to them, pretending they answer to them, asking them rhetorical questions, and pretending to let them speak.

In conclusion, the role of the audience, no matter how unclear its definition is and no matter how silently it receives the various transmissions without always being able to react in real time, remains very serious and crucial not only for the development of a communication event but also for the continuation and the good quality of the relationship between transmitter and receiver on the level of the media.

PART II

THE ATTITUDE OF FICTIVE SYMPATHY

2

The Vernacularization
of Media Discourse[1]

2.1 Mimicking the Informal Register

FOR THE PAST YEARS, and especially after the reconstitution of Greek democracy in 1974, journalists have been using a new language that is more approachable, popular, and entrapping but also firmly attached to its essence in an almost authoritarian way. This language gives the impression of a product characterized by its popular characteristics rather than its words and style. The phenomenon of copying and appropriating the informal register of citizens by people with authority, at the level of vocabulary, can be attributed to the fact that, at the end of the twentieth and mostly in the beginning of the twenty-first century, radio and television—given the wide range in which they can transmit information—attempted to popularize their general presence and to give access to a live and attractive source of information to millions of listeners and viewers.

The mass media acquired both an informational and a political power. The reinforcement of their power—a result of "liberating" privatization—turned them into strong centers of authority and decision-making, and they essentially started to intervene in the relationship between political authority and the people, thus weakening the former (Peponis 2006). It was inevitable that their intervention and reinforcement would also be evident in the language they used.

At the same time, the intensity shown in their commercial operation, together with the simultaneous bombardment and almost imperialist dominance of advertising, resulted in a situation where the media audience was not treated as an audience made up of citizens but as an audience made up of consumers. This

---

[1] Important elements of this chapter that are presented here revised and enriched first appeared in my doctoral dissertation and in my book *The Popular Language of the News: An Attitude of Illusive Intimacy* (2006).

was the outcome of the operation of the information and communication sectors that were developed in the past decades in a very harsh and demanding free market. Their operation as businesses reinforced the element of entertainment, thus influencing in multiple ways the form and content of the media themselves.[2] Besides, many versions of media discourse were not far away from a theatrical synthesis, where the spectacle and theatricality were prominent.

In order for the elements of popularized news, which served the commercial purpose of media companies as well as the ideologies of their owners, to reach their recipients/consumers, media discourse would have to adjust accordingly and to appear more and more vernacularized, easily understood, and therefore intentionally sympathetic and accessible to its audience. Thus, it would not disturb the microcosm of its recipients and would additionally offer them a kind of euphoria since the language norm they use, even in its most vernacular variations, is not stigmatized but elevated, which on its own can provide an element of contentment and pleasure (Fiske 2000:459–460). These are necessary elements for maintaining a state of passivity, which the media tried to establish with, among other things, the uncontrollable use of the image against linguistic expression.

The sectors of media discourse attempted to convince their audience that they spoke just like the people next door and that they considered their viewers/listeners special, which genuinely appealed to the audience (for example, "the people prefer to watch us every day," "we answer to our audience," "we interpret the public sentiment," "we are here because you asked us to be here," and so on). By considering their audiences as potential and contested, the mass media entered a daily and truly exhausting competition with all the means at their disposal (language, audiovisual means), trying to guess intentions and expectations, likes and dislikes, and trying to draw the citizens/consumers' interest (Fiske 2000:455). They tried to achieve "acceptability" (Koutsoulelou-Michou 1997:155) of journalistic expression given the fact that democratic legitimacy based on language form was axiomatically reserved for the transmitter of media discourse. The use of a vernacularized language and the overuse of positive connotations could coerce the receivers into thinking that the journalist sent out accurate messages that would be, most importantly, relevant to their own interests, positions, desires, and expectations.

I would argue that since 1974, this new journalistic language has followed the "new language" of politics, "a language equally authoritarian to the older

---

[2]   During the memoranda period in Greece, the number of news shows on many radio stations was reduced and they were replaced by music shows. The reason was that the news—especially regarding the financial measures taken by the government—was scary for the listeners and made them less prone to consuming radio news shows.

one, however more entrapping, because the historical language question bequeathed it a connotation of progressive beliefs" (Fragkoudaki 1999:209-213). This is a language that allowed the representatives of authority to transmit their progressive ideas in words, not speeches, thus offering in such a form political attributes that, in any other case, would have to be conveyed through content. And although one would hope that journalistic language should only serve the needs of the recipients regarding information, news, proof, and analysis of facts, it tends to replace the aforementioned functions with exaggeration, sensationalism, and sophistry. It has been suggested that this kind of imposition could very well have the traits of *extreme violence* (Fragkoudaki 1999:209-213).

Having analyzed the symbolisms of the demotic language on a public level during the past decades,[3] I claim that new representations that resulted from certain intentions and outlooks were added to the portrayals of language. The use of the demotic language—or the vernacular, as we like to call it—symbolized the end of formality in public discourse, and the consequences were interesting. A systematic use of the vernacular for the shaping of public opinion has been observed. The newer and modern "demoticists" that came from the existing political and publishing hierarchies showed interest in approaching the lower middle class through the vernacularization of the language code and with a de novo use of dialectal elements not only in media and political discourses but also in advertising discourse.[4]

The symbolism regarding the demotic language was caused by a revolutionary attitude, but it has subsequently been associated with the efforts of those in power to convince the masses that they are friends of the people and are socially sensitive. On the other hand, the wide use of the vernacular during the movement of indignados in Greece solidifies the position that the demotic remains a timeless and indisputable emblem of revolutionary attitude, antiauthoritarianism, and of genuine interest in the real concerns of the people, as opposed to what the hierarchies claim is in the interest of the people.[5] As a result, even though the emblematization of language remains strong, it nevertheless changes fields, given that crucial ideological and cultural points of departure shift towards different centers of power and wealth. Thus, portrayals of the demotic language and the vernacular can be saved by diversifying them through their enrichment with new and contemporary dimensions.

---

[3] See also the Bibliography, Section C for a link to a PDF of a paper on this topic presented by me, A. Lygoura, and D. Sakatzis.

[4] See also Tsitsanoudis-Mallidis, N. and E. Theodoropoulos 2015:211-237.

[5] However, as we will see in Chapter Three, when the country entered the memoranda period, the demotic language was used for different reasons.

Considering that the language of mass media is characterized by ideological undercurrents or is even stigmatized by them, I examined the artificial creation of an attitude that I initially called *attitude of fictive sympathy*. What interested me was not solely the vocabulary but also the register, which I believed would aim to cover the distance and the difference between the dominant group and the dominated citizens. In other words, it would attempt to reduce the distance between the two extremities of a theoretically unified schema with paternalistic relations of power on one end and relationships of solidarity and familiarity on the other. Closing this considerable gap could be facilitated by mixing the public/impersonal/functional sphere with the private/domestic/emotional one.

Furthermore, by accepting Dizelos's (1976:98) relatively old view that journalists become inventors every time they want to transmit some social information to the community—a view that is founded on the Chomskian analysis of the creative use of language—I thought that it would be scientifically interesting to examine the scale of inventiveness required by fictive sympathy to bring convincing and expected results. In this context, it would be extremely interesting to study the various language choices through which social reality was beautified, idealized or even distorted, falsified, and obscured (Fowler 1991; Fairclough 1995). These processes happen through the utilization of the modalities of language and the appeal to emotions that can blur impressions and human judgment.

In the chapters that follow, I will attempt to express my positions in regard to the way the attitude of fictive sympathy and illusive intimacy were created through journalistic language, with the aim of making its various messages resonate as much as possible with citizens/consumers.

2.2 Adjusting Speech

In each intervention, speakers have the opportunity to choose among the various language codes, whether acknowledged or cryptic, that may develop within a community and which comprise the communication repertoire. For example, they choose a language code but also their interaction strategy in order to achieve the desired communication outcome with the other members of the community. Their communication skills depend on the level of their skills and knowledge when choosing appropriate alternative codes and modes of communication, depending on the communication conditions and its requirements. The factors that determine this choice can be the following:

- the special characteristics of the speaking participants in communication, such as age, gender, socioeconomic status, profession as well as their interrelationship, such as their degree of familiarity or formality;

- the environment or the general social context within which the conversation or the interaction occurs; the topic—for example, it is possible that some speakers feel more confident talking about a topic using a special language whose terminology they can handle to their satisfaction (Kostoula–Makraki 2001:54–55); and

- previous experiences which have left their mark on a similar communication experience.

According to speech accommodation theory (Kostoula-Makraki 2001:61) and based on Giles et al's claims (1977), the speakers choose, during the communication process, to use a language code that converges with and matches the needs of their interlocutors. If they chose the opposite, it would constitute a conscious divergence and, therefore, a refusal to reinforce their relationship with the representative or representatives of the other language group. It is also possible for the transmission of the message to be delayed. In any case, divergence shows an intention, whether conscious or unconscious, to separate oneself from one's interlocutors.

The convergence is associated with the desire of the speaker to work towards a feeling of unity among people who participate in the conversation, in the context of a kind of affinity between them. According to Giles, Bourhis, and Taylor (1977), the theory of adjustment includes descriptive terms that analyze how speakers adjust communication, the main ones being listed below:

Convergence: the speakers adjust their speech to match the one of their interlocutors on a verbal, morphological, syntactic, or phonetic level.

Divergence: the speakers make changes in their speech that result in their speech being less similar to that of their interlocutors.

Speech maintenance: the speakers do not change their speech but keep it as it was. This phenomenon may be due to caution, skepticism, or even unwillingness on behalf of the speakers to converge towards their interlocutor or interlocutors and, based on that, it could be considered a special type of divergence.

Psychological convergence: the speakers intend to converge their speech towards their interlocutors but, in doing so,[6] they fly off the mark and, in the end, they risk divergence (Kostoula–Makraki 2001:61–62).

---

[6] By overcorrecting, for example.

Coupland and Giles (1988) developed the communication accommodation theory and pointed out the influence of the stereotypical views a speaker has about his/her interlocutors during communication. As a rule, compliance is based on schematic expectations regarding the recipients' communication needs or even shortcomings, something I take seriously into account, especially when I attempt to analyze communication accommodation in relation to agents of media discourse during the past few decades. Giles made a few distinctions, such as upward divergence, downward divergence, upward convergence, and downward convergence, and I will focus mainly on the last one, according to which people with higher status adjust to people with a "lower" one.

2.3 Convergence with the Recipients and Ideological Implications

While applying the abovementioned distinctions to media discourse, I thought it was interesting to look into whether journalists adjust their speech, even at the expense of inspiration, originality, and verbal inventiveness, regarding the language codes of their recipients. I thought it is worth examining if and to what extent they choose, in combination with the respective topics, language codes, and strategies whose goal is to approach the public they address as effectively as possible, thus producing familiar compositions of sounds and images.

The print and electronic media are "typical fields of heteroglossia," since they allow the public—in other words, the many social strata—to access, consume, and produce texts (Georgakopoulou and Goutsos 1999:244). The tendency to mix private and public codes in the press is ever increasing, as is the case for the public character of television with the private—and familiar, I might add—environments (Fairclough 1995). Such practices and attitudes are dictated by the multiple roles of journalism, which often confuses information with spectacle, entertainment, governance, and propaganda.

The interweaving of the public and the private is imprinted, to a certain extent, in the succession of narrative and non-narrative texts, given a narrative tradition that goes back decades (Georgakopoulou and Goutsos 1999). Of course, the "counterattack" of non-narrative texts is also based on the choice of topics that are familiar to recipients. The same researchers (1999:246–247) cited studies of English reality shows and talk shows, according to which the personal testimony of an ordinary person is legitimized as an experience that is worth becoming part of the so-called public sphere (Scannel 1991; Livingstone and Lunt 1994). However, they were cautious about what such a legitimization could signify in a wider ideological context—in other words, whether this transformation of the public sphere constitutes a true reversal of power relations between those who have it and those who do not. This is a question that is still present in the debate to this day.[7]

In my opinion, the convergence between the language employed by the media and by the viewers/listeners and recipients, in general, is not random. I will bring forth an example that is related to the social varieties of language. When journalists adopt a *low language variety* (Mitsis 2000:37), they give the impression that they want to avoid underrating the audience. This is related to a conscious or unconscious desire to prove that they are not attempting a social assessment that undervalues all the variations (social, ethnic varieties) of the national language as being errors and of low quality. If, in other words, journalists manage to give the impression that they deviate from standard speech, the language that has been chosen by the elite for wider communication, then they can also manage to fight and possibly neutralize any suspicions that they are in any way biased against the repertoire of their recipients, who mostly belong to the lower and middle social strata.

The context of this artificial familiarity that is supported by vernacularized repertoires could be based on a common approach by the sectors of discourse and the public. This apparent rapid understanding by the transmitter/journalist is analogous, I would say, to the need for the production of fast and easy conclusions by the reader. This way it is easier to avoid thinking about "strenuous discursive procedures of subversion, mental struggles and emotional pain" (Valiouli 2001:20–21). Such processes are supported "by a person's tendency to predict and expect stereotypical behaviors (predictability principle) and to activate role and person schemas, as well as by its tendency to be based on early, obvious, prominent or impressive, mainly visually, information (early labeling, salience and immediate access principles), as well as existing and frequently used category schemas (accessibility principle)" (Fiske and Taylor 1991:142–147, 177–178).

Based on the above, I made the working hypothesis that while media discourse is by nature formal and public, it employs the low variety on a case-by-case basis, in order to appear popular and familiar to its recipients and to completely close the great distance that divides it from its audiences and recipients. I also hypothesized, and later proved, that the language of journalists followed the language of politicians to a great extent.

For example, the fact that the representatives of the power of the press omitted or even ignored important titles that political personalities held and replaced them with forms of great familiarity is highly interesting.[8] While it

---

[7]   Similar examples can be found in Greek journalistic texts as well.

[8]   Simply *Andreas* for Andreas Papandreou, *Psilos* (i.e. the tall guy) for Konstantinos Mitsotakis, *Alexis* for Alexis Tsipras, and so on.

looked like the press was demystifying the powerful, it was nothing but a trap (1991:213). When used positively, these forms reduce, through a fraudulent familiarity, critical distance and the need for accountability. When used negatively, they assume or undermine critical possibilities. Besides, characterizations and nicknames that gave the impression of *great familiarity* were often used to demean their target.[9]

I believe that a powerful vernacularized language could "camouflage" the means to control public opinion, even the most violent ones. Showing illusive intimacy and fictive sympathy as well as fake affinity to a person or the public itself can weaken and reduce the ability of the audience and the recipients to keep the critical distance they need to keep authority in check or hold it accountable. Journalists accept having negotiable goals, the end one being legitimization, which they develop through virtual grids of intimacy and friendliness towards the recipients, depending each time on their objectives and the dominant group's interests. What is truly happening, however, is that as agents of formal and institutional power, they exercise communicative control on their recipients and their interlocutors by assigning them various roles and positions. Such a strategy makes the powerful appear like they seek the advice of the weak and like they let them decide on their contribution based on predefined roles (Clayman 1991:48–75; Heritage and Greatbatch 1991:93–137; Greatbatch 1992:268–301).[10]

I also suggested that, ever since the 1990s, the agents of media discourse have liked to address their audience with varied elements, thus attempting to show how friendly they have been towards it. Anytime it was appropriate to show respect to the dominant social codes, media discourse used socially appropriate language, apparent respectability, and conservatism. Anytime it was appropriate to show empathy, solidarity, affinity, or even complicity with the audience, the media discourse borrowed from the atypical and non-codified varieties of the national language.

Another reason why media discourse attempted to use popular varieties, against or with the formal, administrative, or national language, was

---

[9] For example: *Giorgakis* (Little George) for Georgios Papandreou, *Kostakis* (Little Kostas) for Kostas Karamanlis, and *Koulis* (Little Kyriakos) for Kyriakos Mitsotakis.

[10] The research on power roles in communication has been expanded to other environments as well, such as those that develop when patients see doctors or therapists or during witness testimonies in courts. Among the topics that have been analyzed are, firstly, the ability to negotiate the formal institutional frameworks with weak participants (patients, for example) in order to create temporary friendly environments with informal character (like, for example, the friendly chat patients have with their doctors) and, secondly, the ways with which the powerful, the agents of authority, attempt temporary reconnection of their intimacy with the recipients of their authority (Georgakopoulou and Goutsos 1999:208).

an intention to appear increasingly youthful and fresh, borrowing elements from the language that young people used, elements that become symbols of youthfulness when they enter the standard vocabulary of a language (Androutsopoulos 2001:108–111). In this way, media discourse gave the impression that it shook off the stereotypical behavior regarding the language of the young, which was supposed to be incomprehensible, diminished, or vulgar. It appeared to be respecting its social, communicative, and psychological causes and characteristics, such as the need for autonomous communications among youth. It also seemed to observe its unconventionality against the appropriate use of the language and the apparent respectability, which usually characterizes teenagers' lives. Of course, this attitude by the media also served commercial purposes, since young audiences are of strong commercial interest.

2.4 The Calculated Anti-Authoritative Aspect of Fictive Sympathy

At the level of language, showing an attitude of fictive sympathy is, in my opinion, both moderated and controlled. I attribute this to the fact that the media are themselves part of the establishment; as a result, no uncontrolled or extreme challenge can be accepted or justified. Should this happen, it would be equivalent to an auto-negation of the medium as agent of language—and thus of the medium itself. There are many tools to achieve a convincing and functional style towards the audience, such as the use of popular idioms, turns of phrase, or even taboo words. These seem to oppose the apparent respectability but only to the extent of an artificially reserved criticism towards hierarchy. Their use can explore the limits of audacity as well as the refusal of social structures and values. However, it cannot exceed the designated limits.

Discourse can rarely be subversive regarding the dominant class or various dominant groups, television viewers included. According to Chatzisavvidis, whenever such a thing has been attempted, discourse has ended up being "self-negated as a social event" (2000:102). This is because, as mediating discourse, it is a product of its own means of production—in other words, the media. And whether these belong to the public or the private sector, they are connected to financial profit and political influence (Gotovos 1996:111–116). For both these parameters to function, they need a large number of recipients for the transmitted messages, either on the level of popularity, opinion formation, and propaganda or on the level of commercial value. In order for the viewers, listeners, or readers to multiply, depending on the case, the producers of media discourse have to adjust the messages they transmit to the desires, intentions, stereotypes, and general ideology of their recipients. If they do not, they have to convince or coerce their recipients into thinking that they did, through the attitude of fictive sympathy.

No medium of authority is self-immolating. Even when the messages transmitted through media discourse give the impression that they undermine the status quo or the dominant class, this subversion is manifested in a controlled way and only appears to express the demands of the middle or lower classes, without making them rise or mobilizing them to stand against authority or to initiate a possible redistribution of power.

In such a case, media discourse attempts to describe and, at the same time, to relieve tensions and situations, appearing as a friend or sympathizer of the masses, who also are its recipients. But, in reality, it has already chosen sides as mediator and mediated, as it is bound by the owners of the channels used for its transmission since its existence relies on the approval and legitimization of the latter. For example, it is rare to see journalists go against the desires and positions of their recipients.[11] Likewise, we will never see or hear sectors of media discourse disparage or insult their audience. Similarly, however, it is uncommon to see journalists going against the interests of those who own and control the medium where they're employed and through which they can transmit their messages.[12] On the contrary, there are examples of shows that were cut while on air because the producers/hosts tried to talk subversively and against the interests of the dominant group.

These phenomena can be better interpreted if we consider the fact that media discourse stems not from a transmitter (the person that talks or signs a journalistic text) but from a multifaceted and hierarchical agent (Politis 2001:115). It's at best naive to believe that media discourse is produced solely by one person. Before its transmission or publication, it has been checked by a host of people (editors, directors, owners, publishers), either regarding content—i.e. if it's congruent with and serves the ideological orientation of the medium and its owners—or regarding style, form, and general organization. Behind everyone and everything, there are the owners of the medium—public or private—who may not always intervene preventively or repressively on a daily basis during the production of the journalistic text, but they have dictated in advance the identity and ideology (the "line") of the medium. Its owners and the journalists are obligated to follow that line so they can continue to be employed.

---

[11] This was not true in various broadcasts the days before the July 5, 2015, referendum. The question was whether to accept the agreement plan of the three institutions—the European Commission, the European Central Bank, and the International Monetary Fund—that was proposed to Greece on June 25. The rejection of the proposal received 61.31 percent of the votes. For more on the memorandum language, see Chapter Three.

[12] There are rare exceptions, however, mostly in public radio and television and even more rarely in private radio and television.

2.5 The Service of High Orality

Another element that serves the cultivation of the attitude of fictive sympathy is *high orality*. Some of the characteristics of orality that can be seen in media discourse these past few decades are: deficiencies, use of words from everyday language, repetitions, gaps, use of stereotypical expressions, use of ambiguous and achromatic words (Babiniotis 1994:196), unmotivated change of grammatical person during the speech, reference to things or objects that are present during the speech, delayed completion or correction, intervention, change from indirect to direct speech, and lack of a rigid textual structure.[13] The similarity between media discourse and oral speech has now been solidified. Media discourse has appropriated many elements from everyday oral speech and is increasingly becoming a typical sample of private speech and not of public speech while there is also an increasing tendency to adopt *conversationalization* from the British media (Valiouli 2001:10).

Furthermore, media discourse frequently attempts to avoid word-hunting, grandiloquence, and other elements that could be associated with the literacy of the official norms compared to the directness of communicative completeness of popular variations.

However, there is no certainty of the association of high orality with journalese (Valiouli 2001:18). The term *journalese* is used disparagingly, despite the fact that it has to do with a language variety that is dominant and possesses power. In other words, journalists do not follow the rules of written media discourse which, in the case of pure news, allow them to present only the facts but, rather, embellish their texts with emotionally charged words or phrases and with assessments through which they express their own opinions and interpretations.

In conclusion, the fact that media discourse, both printed and electronic, adopts high orality can be attributed to its goal of becoming familiar and understood by the recipients as fast and as easily as possible in order to influence them significantly. The viewers, listeners, or readers of such a discourse feel safer when the image and the status of their own language world is not disturbed, so they might become relatively gullible regarding the categorizations and assessments that are proposed. Besides, such a thought process

---

[13] Orwell (1999) says: "So did the fact of having very few words to choose from. Relative to our own, the Newspeak vocabulary was tiny, and new ways of reducing it were constantly being devised. Newspeak, indeed, differed from most all other languages in that its vocabulary grew smaller instead of larger every year. Each reduction was a gain, since the smaller the area of choice, the smaller the temptation to take thought. Ultimately it was hoped to make articulate speech issue from the larynx without involving the higher brain centres at all."

regarding categorizations can quickly lead to probable inferences despite the absence of sufficient true data as far as size, relativity, and quality are concerned (Fiske and Taylor 1991:382–384).

2.6 Fictive Sympathy or Extreme Conformity?

Should the aforementioned aspects and manifestations of fictive sympathy simply be treated as the speakers' tendencies for overcompliance and adjustment in front of their audiences? Such a hypothesis could be added to the plethora of scientific views that have turned away from the static perception of recipients as passive and could function as one more confirmation of the view that the recipients are active co-creators of communication as per Bakhtin (1981). Planning one's speech according to the audience is a topic that has been studied scientifically by communication accommodation theory (Coupland and Giles 1988).

Just like social workers, for instance, over-adjust their speech depending on the communication needs and weaknesses of their elderly recipients (with repetitions, simplifications, explanations, and paralinguistic elements such as slow and loud speech), we could argue that, in the same way, journalists plan and adjust their speech depending on the communication needs of their audience or of a part of it, based on various qualitative statistical studies and market research available to them or to the directors of the medium they work for. Journalists are relatively coerced into behaving in a certain way, to the extent that their shows should have sufficient viewers in an extremely competitive market, so that shows in question can both serve commercial interest—as far as advertisers are concerned—and shape public opinion.[14]

2.7 The Research Challenge

What was also added to my research interests were the evening news broadcasts on national TV stations and not the various political shows that were on TV at various times throughout the day. I made this choice because news broadcasts are considered to be highly prestigious (Fiske 2000:413).[15] I then examined the

---

[14] Here it would be prudent to mention other parameters that should be seriously considered and which form the shape of media discourse, such as the parameters of ethnic origins for a group of people (defined by common historical origins, common language and culture, and possibly common religion) but also of gender.

[15] As proof of their social responsibility, media companies that want to issue or renew their TV licenses mention news broadcasts and other political shows.

evidence that emerged through a series of interviews with the hosts of these evening news broadcasts but also with journalists that were active participants in how the news broadcasts are presented.

While conducting research for this distinguished part of media discourse, the power of the theoretical view that media discourse, and especially television discourse, acquires more and more elements from the vernacular was empirically substantiated with various outlooks. The reasons, as I have already mentioned, can be commercial (advertising), propagandistic (formation of ideology, manufacture of consent), along with other possibilities such as an effort to conceal the major power this particular medium has.

It has already been stated that there are plenty of journalists that use media discourse as a weapon with which to convince their audiences that they speak like "people next door," despite the fact that media discourse mainly uses an ideological language since those who use it are representatives of a very powerful authority. Thus, although media discourse keeps its authoritative function almost entirely intact (Chatzisavvidis 2000:40), I noticed that during the past decades, and especially since the restoration of democracy in 1974, it did attempt to shed the mantle of an agent of the powers that be and get closer, at least in its form, to the popular linguistic standards of its recipients.

While conducting my research, I examined how modern television discourse attempted to give the impression that it can distance itself from the public and official role of the superior, the expert, and the agent of generally dominant rules regarding ostensibly respectable speech. What was also examined was the extent to which such an attitude provides the possibility to express feelings of solidarity, intimacy, and complicity towards its audience and also to possibly appear like it is questioning the hierarchy and the dominance of reason over emotions. This attitude, which I call *attitude of fictive sympathy* or *highly fictive sympathy* or *illusive intimacy*, is based on the use of the vernacular and on a language that is easily understood by the recipients. That language makes it possible for the representatives of the power of the press to prove and exhaust their progressiveness and social awareness with words and to appear as if they are abolishing or trying to abolish (and reconcile) the conflict of interests between an oligarchical dominant class and the crowds of dominated citizens. This happens because such a language gives its users goods and qualities that in any other case would have to be earned, not through form, but through content. The research questions I mainly dealt with were the following:

A. Is there a so-called attitude of fictive sympathy by the agents of television discourse against the audience and, if so, how is it created and where is it based? How is it expressed on a language level?

B. What are the goals of such an attitude and how does it influence its recipients?

C. What is the meaning of the attempt by the agents of media discourse to close the distance between formal/public and informal/private discourse as far as journalistic language is concerned?

D. What do the agents of media discourse say about how journalistic language has adjusted to the communication repertoire of the recipients and the reasons that impose such a change?

E. How does the television audience react to such a language? Does it consider it as proof of progressiveness and social awareness by the agents of media discourse and the media in general or does it have reservations as it is now more suspicious than in the past?

In order to find answers to these questions and with the general principles of sociolinguistics as my basic tools, I researched television discourse as it is transmitted through evening news broadcasts from various TV stations in Greece, researching both how the hosts and the reporters speak and what speech is like during television interviews. I then acquired more data for this research by conducting interviews with the agents of media discourse—evening news hosts and journalists that participated in how the news broadcasts are presented by appearing as commentators, etc.—in an effort to record their positions and reactions as transmitters of media discourse. The recipients and the television viewers were not excluded from my citation of the answers gathered from a questionnaire I gave to an approximately representative sample of recipients.

2.7.1 Critical discourse analysis

My research approach was based on the principles of critical discourse analysis, which focuses on the ways in which sociocultural and ideological practices correspond to language. I treated texts as language units with meanings and submeanings that form and represent certain situations which are externally determined by, and then determine, social and cultural contexts. I attempted to show the external pressures of the environments on the formation not just of the textual units' content but also on the forms that are chosen, depending on the communicative situation and the wider sociopolitical environment. What really stood out in my research was the admission that language substance does not always occur effortlessly or spontaneously, but it may be preprepared and predefined in its organization and structure by the dominant norms, ideologies, and public authority structures, which are primarily interested in their conservation and perpetuation.

Media discourse has been studied as a vibrant, depicting field of ideological roles and schemas, with language being treated as an instrument of authority, control, and social shaping of reality (Georgakopoulou and Goutsos 1999:205). Fairclough (1995) talks about communication practices that are characterized by a lack of transparency, which results in the fact that the recipients of various texts cannot realize which ideologies they serve and which dangers their reproduction brings. Therefore, this is about an ideology that is not explicitly and loudly expressed but is present in a more implicit way. Some of the elements modern research has focused on are the following:

- the ways in which texts cultivate and reproduce power relations and relations of socio-political or cultural hegemony by choosing certain words or syntax;

- the element of modality as a mechanism that expresses the struggle between ideological systems (Kress 1996:15–31; Van Leeuwen 1996:32–70); and

- the ways in which journalists, as agents of a legitimized power (Georgakopoulou and Goutsos 1999:208), exert communication influence on their guests during an interview and also the ways in which agents of authority create their roles or attempt to ephemerally befriend and acquire the trust of the participants in communication or the recipients of their speech.

Finally, I believe that, despite the harsh criticism we hear from time to time that critical discourse analysis leaves out oral communication and focuses on written speech too much, or that it lacks effective suggestions to reduce textual chauvinism, or even that it uses hegemonic, rigid, and scientific language, it is still a powerful method and a great tool of discourse analysis which has proven extremely useful to modern researchers.

2.7.2 Databases and data

The present research was based on two pillars. The first one had to do with amassing data—that is, pieces of speech as articulated by the agents of journalistic power as authorized by society through a certain selection of samples of media discourse coming from evening news broadcasts (called *central news broadcasts* in Greece) of the national TV stations with the most viewers. The second one consisted of interviewing the agents of media discourse themselves and asking them to answer specific questions as dictated by my research. The research material was completed from the recording of the answers of a representative sample of TV viewers who were asked to answer a relevant questionnaire.

Further, the corpus of news texts came from the evening news broadcasts of the Greek TV stations with the most viewers, based on measurements conducted by the polling company AGB Hellas during the years 2004 and 2005. The exclusive source of materials for this study was the four most viewed central news broadcasts on Greek television. These were: Mega Events (Mega Γεγονότα), Antenna News (Τα Νέα του Antenna), Alpha News (Alpha Ειδήσεις) and Alter News Bulletin (Κεντρικό Δελτίο Alter).[16]

The collected material was composed of words and phrases taken from:

a. report announcements by the hosts of the evening news broadcasts and also comments by journalists during the broadcast, either by the central host or by the journalists that actively participated in presenting the broadcast, whether they were permanent participants or guests;

b. visualized titles of reports that were transmitted by the news broadcasts and phrases used as titles during conversations among journalists; and

c. excerpts of statements, comments, judgments and analyses by journalists and ordinary citizens that were heard and transmitted during these news broadcasts from December 28, 2004, to March 23, 2005.

As for excerpts taken from statements made by ordinary citizens, eyewitnesses, disaster victims, and other complainants, what was considered was the role of edited shots that came before a report.[17] The time frame within which the news broadcasts were recorded was one that included some major news.[18]

---

[16] The TV station Alter (formerly Channel 5) is not in operation today. The TV station Mega has resumed operation after a break.

[17] According to Filippakis (2004), the task of inserting a desired statement or some piece of correspondence by a journalist within a report is a decision that is made with the editor of each news broadcast.

[18] Some of the topics the news broadcasts mostly dealt with were the revelations about corruption within the church and the justice system, farmer mobilization, the deadly tsunami in Asia and its aftermath, the law about the principal shareholders, the financial crisis, price increases, new taxes and the difficult situation Greek households are finding themselves in, the neglect of the Greek countryside and border islands, the lack of state health services, Greek-Turkish relations, intragovernmental problems, and arguments within the opposition party of New Democracy, etc.

2.8 Discussion of Data Drawn from TV News Broadcasts

Utilizing audio and video recordings from the news broadcasts, I segmented these journalistic texts in order to analyze individual parts that I approached as *chunks of human behavior* (Grimes 1975:21) and as occasional *cultural data* that serve a particular ideological orientation.

Based on the fundamental assertion that language does not automatically and mechanically reflect reality but instead creates it, I have attempted to answer the question of whether grids of authority and of sociopolitical or cultural hegemony are constructed through texts by the agents of journalistic authority, whether short-lived and fictitious bonds of friendship and trust with the recipients of media discourse are attempted, or whether both can happen at the same time.

In particular, by bringing up certain examples, I have attempted to substantiate my view of the development of an attitude of fictive sympathy or highly illusive intimacy, whose goal is to make media discourse appear like it is serving the interests of the people. In other words, its goal is to appear as serving the interests of those who belong to social groups that lack authority and are summoned as consumers, even though they might not always react in this way. They have their own cultural forms and interests that are often in opposition to those that belong to the producers of cultural and commercial goods (Fiske 2000:455).

Besides the presentation of information and of the news, the goal is to make propaganda easier and to manufacture, or even impose, consent on public opinion. The news broadcasts' goal is also to widen and retain an audience of appropriate size and composition so that media discourse will be in demand as a commercial good, which can then be sold to advertisers.

My research showed that the creation of an attitude of fictive sympathy is shown on a language level through the following practices by:

- using words and phrases that belong to the vernacular but also of geographic and social varieties;

- bringing (and upgrading) the private element within the public element and attempting to remove the distance between the private/personal and the public/impersonal;

- implicitly expressing the ideology of dissent and pretending to be in ideological alliance with the public;

- promoting emotions over reason; and
- covering popular topics in news broadcasts.

2.8.1 The use of the vernacular

The observed use of vernacular words and phrases, which was not extensive but reasonable and occasional, in combination with a mix of narrative and non-narrative elements, led me to believe initially that the producers of such media discourse tried to become familiar and approachable to their audience. Through the use of vernacular words and phrases, the news function of media is easier to achieve, in parallel with the propagandistic one, which attempts to influence the recipients into adopting a certain opinion, attitude, or ideology.

Media discourse converges toward the typical everyday language of the lower and middle classes from which the majority of the audience originates. Thus, many elements are adopted from everyday speech, resulting in a speech that appears to be private rather than public (Valiouli 2001).

Besides, according to Giles's speech accommodation theory, the speaker, during communication, chooses to use a language code that converges and matches with the needs of the interlocutor since, if the opposite were chosen, this would be a conscious divergence and a possible refusal to reinforce the links with the representative of the other language group (Kostoula-Makraki 2001:61). Under this light, the convergence is associated with the speakers'—in this case, the agents of media discourse—desire to create a feeling of unity between themselves and the people who participate in the conversation—in this case the recipients of media discourse, the audience—in an effort to cultivate an affinity of sorts between them.

The attempt to make the journalistic language of television more vernacularized is betrayed by the selective use of certain geographic and social variations, despite the shared opinion that the development of media limits various dialects in structural and functional ways (Setatos 1978). And while media discourse appears as a mechanism that drives language to a homogeneity (Chatzisavvidis 2000:37), I found, however, that in specific cases and for specific reasons, it appropriates words and phrases from various language varieties (Mitsis 1999:31, 46, 91–92) and that these variations are both *geographic* and *social* (οι ξενέρωτοι or "the uncool," οι δήθεν or "the pretentious," με λάντζα οι νεφροπαθείς στη Λέρο or "kidney patients wash dishes in Leros," and so on). I found that this always happens when the topics reported are considered "light" (for instance, spicy love stories, topics about how youth have fun, everyday problems, etc.) without excluding the use of the vernacular in cases that can be characterized as serious and which are about people or institutions that are considered prestigious (for example, the prime minister's public appearances, an intragovernmental crisis, Greek-Turkish relations, and so on). The reappearance of dialectal elements observed in advertising is of great importance as well.[19]

In addition to geographic and social variations, I also observed the use of *allolects* (language of the other) (Fragkoudaki 1999:63–64) and *idiolects*, which are languages used by a person or a limited number of people such as a group of friends or a family (Dictionary of Standard Greek 2001:606). It would be naive to think that showing such a word, which has been uttered by an ordinary person, to the mass of viewers (for example, έχει πέσει νεκραΐλα στην αγορά which roughly translates to "the market is dead") is a random occurrence.

This is due to the fact that, after all the footage has been collected at the news department of a TV station, what follows is the editing process conducted by journalists and other executive staff. It is often a painstaking process since each report does not get much airtime (one or two minutes at best), which means that they have to select the footage using strict criteria. When such a neologism or morpheme that cannot even be found in dictionaries is transmitted by a news broadcast, it is possible that it will be reinforced and start to be used by other recipients. I attribute the fact that the news editor and the reporter decide to air this neologism to the conscious or unconscious desire to give the impression that they respect the idiolect of a citizen and, by extension, his or her personality as an individual. Today, social media have a significant role in how neologisms are propagated.[20]

Furthermore, along with the use of scientific and technical terminology (cloning, globalization, the internet) which points to the idea of a rigidly scientific and technocratic spirit, I have also observed a simultaneous effort to simplify various scientific and technical terms (for example, the overindebtedness of households was also described using slang words such as φέσια and βερεσέδια and government farming subsidies were described with the phrase θα τους σκάσει τα λεφτά, which is a slang expression for "they will be paid," and so

---

[19] In a recent paper that I published (2015), I recorded a powerful reappearance of dialectal varieties in modern advertising discourse and discussed the attitudes against language as they appear in language used in printed and electronic media as well as the internet. Despite the sociocultural tendency to homogenize the use of language, I observed that in the planning phase of advertising messages there is use of speech items with a dialectal form, which more widely embraces geographic varieties. The recruitment of dialectal varieties, which are often changed or modified, is done in a jocular manner and aims to attract the recipient's attention. I concluded, however, that the presence of dialects in advertising provides elements that will help them persevere but does not work as a pool from which dialectal elements can be drawn, nor is it a safe way for them to proliferate.

[20] For more on this and how they are established with fast-track processes, see also Tsitsanoudis-Mallidis 2018.

on). The fact that various technical or scientific terms get simplified betrays a conscious or even unconscious tendency of journalists to dissociate themselves from phenomena of lingual or cultural hegemony. By avoiding the use of technical or scientific terms, they attempt to make their speech easily and quickly understood by the mass of recipients and especially by those social groups that do not have access to scientific or technical language. If they adopted a specialized language at all times, their speech would acquire or maintain elements of cultural hegemony and there would also be a risk of characterizing its recipients as inferior.

Another thing that is worth including in the conversation has to do with the observed wide use of homonymous words and phrases, what we usually call clichés: for example, κόντρα which denotes a fight; μαϊμού which literally means "monkey" but denotes a knockoff product and is used alongside other words to point to various illegitimate products and services such as ταξί-μαϊμού (fake taxis) and άδειες-μαϊμού (fake licenses); λίστα which means "list"; and others. The almost systematic use of these stereotypical words and phrases, which are in danger of losing their exact meaning because they are used so often, should not, in my opinion, be solely attributed to journalists' poor vocabulary as Tzannetakos suggests (n.d.). I believe this phenomenon is the result of a general effort by the agents of media discourse to adopt an intimate and conversational style towards the viewer, using words and phrases that match the language repertoire of the majority of the recipients and do not disturb the image they have formed about what language is really like.

2.8.2 Private made public

According to Fiske (2000:418), the news belongs to the public sphere[21] and not the private sphere. The private element appears only when there is a topic that disturbs normality—in other words, when it disturbs law and order, like in the case of a brutal crime or a great success. However, these past few years, I have found that a citizen's personal testimony can become a topic of deep concern for the public space and thus can enter the public sphere (Scannel 1991; Livingstone and Lunt 1994). This was made easier by reality shows that familiarized the audience with the idea of being watched.

In the data I explored, it was very easy for citizens' testimonies to be transferred to the public sphere, especially when it came to topics such as the market's high prices (γεμίσαμε βερεσέδια and γράφουμε στα τεφτέρια,

---

[21] According to Tulloch and Moran (1986:239), drama is mainly occupied with the private, emotional, and domestic sphere, while news broadcasts, political shows, and documentaries are more about the public sphere.

both slang expressions meaning "selling with credit"), the ramifications the various government policies have on citizens (εδώ είμαστε ένα μάτσο χάλια which roughly translates to "everything here is a mess"), and the neglect of the countryside in terms of infrastructure with undertones of antiauthoritarianism (οι πολιτικοί μας τάζουν αρνιά και φλασκιά which is an expression about big promises that never came true, literally translated as "the politicians promise us lambs and bottles"). The opinions of unknown and anonymous citizens became elevated, since the editing team of news broadcasts chose their quotes as titles for various reports (a report on the mobilizations of the farmers was titled "Άντε στην υγειά μας και καλό αγώνα!" meaning "To our good health, for a good fight!"). The fact that the testimony's inclusion in the public sphere would be respected by the media and the dialect though which this testimony was expressed with its simultaneous use of sayings and folk proverbs is not a rare phenomenon, for example: Όταν τον γερούτσι ο καλόηρος να τον χτυπήσ', αυτός έκανι πίσου and Άλλαξι η Μανωλιός κι έβαλι τη σκούφια αλλιώς, the former talking about being cautious and the latter about people not being able to change despite appearances. Even the use of idiosyncrasies, neologisms, or even elements that belong to the citizens' allolects would be adopted and transmitted.

It was not only the citizens' testimonies and experiences that had a place in the public sphere but also the private moments of politicians as well as celebrities from the entertainment industry.[22] I observed that on the one hand, the citizens' testimonies and experiences were elevated to the public sphere (elevation of the informal and private to the public); and on the other hand, the projection of an image in which the representatives of the public sphere/the agents of authority appeared to be adjusting to the recipients' routines (descent of the formal and public into the private).

This is an interweaving of the private and the public and an organized attempt to constitute a collective identity within society that hides or conceals the existing differences.

Alongside the use of bookish words (όλεθρος and ολίσθημα meaning "devastation" and "sideslip" respectively), which add respectability and validity to media discourse, idioms such as ο πρωθυπουργός έγινε τούρμπο and έφαγε τα μουστάκια του, both slang expressions meaning how angry someone became with the former referring to the prime minister himself (an equivalent

---

[22] An example of this was the way the news described a visit by the then prime minister Kostas Karamanlis, his wife Natasha, and their baby twins to an amusement park in Rafina on January 2, 2005. In this case, the news showed images from the powerful couple's everyday life, even though the images themselves betrayed none of that power since these were activities that were particularly familiar to the recipients/audience.

expression, albeit not literal, would be "he went haywire") are also used, which push the systematic institution of hierarchy in media discourse downwards. While the distance between the recipients of media discourse from its authorized agents and transmitters is certain due to the authoritative function, sometimes we get the impression that the hierarchy is challenged. Conversations use an informal everyday language which is familiar and friendly to the audience, whose language repertoire is neither rejected nor challenged, both vertically and horizontally (socially or geographically)—for example, σε πιάνω instead of σε καταλαβαίνω ("I get you" instead of "I understand you"), έχει γούστο ο παπάς instead of είναι χαριτωμένος ("the priest is rad" instead of "he's pleasant"), καλός για να πας στα μπουζούκια μαζί του ("good for a fun night out"), etc.

The inclusion of the private in the public space raises the question of whether it is connected to a true reversal of power relations between those who have authority and those who do not. In my opinion, the legitimization of bringing the testimony of an ordinary person to the public sphere and the use of elements that belong to the everyday life of agents of authority are associated with an effort to remove distances separating those who have power and those who do not. More specifically, I ascribe the journalists' efforts to bring citizens' testimonies to the public sphere to an attempt to form new relations among the agents of journalistic discourse and their recipients, with the former experimenting with being friendly and trying to connect with the audiences for reasons that have already been mentioned multiple times.

Indeed, the use of an everyday, vernacular language, as much as it is possible, facilitates the partial and occasional reduction of distances that separate the viewer from the producer/transmitter of media discourse and, by extension, the populous group to which the recipients of such discourse belong from the relatively small group of the agents of journalistic power.

This attempt includes the various live debates, especially those with audience participation. During those debates, there is a frequent use of the vernacular and the journalists are on a first-name basis, aiming to give the impression that the viewers are watching, perhaps even in secret, an unofficial, private conversation among people that are similar to them and are acquainted with one another, as they confess their various thoughts. Consequently, everything that is heard is supposedly not prepared in advance but is reliable and effortlessly sincere.

2.8.3 Implicit expression of ideology

The expression of ideology through media discourse can often occur implicitly, as it is codified within the choice of grammar and vocabulary of the journalists themselves or is dispersed within the submeanings shared by the transmitter and the receiver. A hierarchically created political and social reality is able not only to be depicted but also reproduced through language. Language is transformed into a great tool of control of public opinion. We cannot just talk about an *ideological function of language* but about an *ideological language* per se. The ideological language can serve the manufacturing of acceptance and consent but can also impose it by shrinking or nullifying the role of the recipient and by undermining the polarity of the dialogue. The ideological language can also elevate the recipients by appealing to the importance of their role.

The dominant monologue takes the place of the dialogue, and it is legitimized or even normalized, dressed as it is with characteristics that entrap the recipients, limit them to silence and passive acceptance, and decrease their confidence in being able to bring about changes by challenging what is being imposed on them. At the same time, the powerful transmitter is protected from the dangers of a critical response to the messages it transmits, as well as from the natural subsequent criticism. Language is imposed as self-evident through pluralism and axiological elements and is proven as reliable. More specifically:

- The (sometimes systematic) use of vernacularized expression and the high frequency of certain types and rhetorical repetitions point to a pluralistic media discourse. The various axiological expressions that can be heard against those who doubt the uniqueness and objectivity of the description of an event point to the same pluralistic discourse as well.

- Media discourse on TV, as is expressed in news broadcasts, is characterized by an axiological character and form, since hidden within vocabulary and syntax are judgments and assessments of people and things, which constrain—if not coerce—the recipient into not doubting what seems self-explanatory and self-evident. Words and phrases such as *country, people, nation, the people's interests, citizen,* etc. are not just used by politicians but also by journalists, whose goal it is to send out a message that does not need justification and proof.

- Furthermore, there is often evidence of a media discourse which, because of the position that its producers/transmitters/agents have, is self-evident since it transmits messages, which are considered a priori true and irrefutable. Phrases such as "informed sources," "according to verified information," or "well-informed circles say" are used as pools of legitimacy and validity in which media discourse is immersed. There are also frequent euphemistic phrases since journalists and the media they work for are self-described as "impartial," "independent," "reliable," "free," "objective," and so on.

- It's also interesting to see the use of certain pronouns. For example, "we" is sometimes used to represent an ideological congruence between the journalist and the public, which is generally unjustifiable, since it is only found on the level of the form of words and not in their content. Such an alliance is underlined by the use of "they," which is utilized to point to any visible or invisible "rival alliance" that can be the political authority or any other kind of power besides the journalists'.

Besides the implicit expression of ideology or the implicit challenge against the status quo by the agents of media discourse, it is possible to trace, within a not necessarily proven ideological alliance with the recipients, examples of explicit challenges against the dominant class and especially against the political ruling class. There are various textual items where a clear reaction is depicted against authoritative structures and institutions. In cases of explicit challenges against the ruling class by journalists, who claim that it is not an "I" that speaks but a "we," there are seeds of revolt and subversion of the current power distribution, especially when the phrases used have an almost derisive and ironic tone. Media discourse is seemingly in agreement with a classless contract to disturb the status quo and the powers that are derived from it and, at the same time, as if it distances itself from adhering to the contract's terms, given the fact that it does not give up the authoritative elements that are inherent to it.

2.8.4 The domination of emotion

There are certain data points where I have noticed that language is imprinted with a certain kind of domination or an attempt to dominate, of emotions over reason. I have also noticed that through the use of the vernacular, or of a vernacularized language, there is an attempt to express emotions of affection, despair as well as ironic and audacious attitudes against the dominant class and its structures. Phrases such as τρελαίνομαι με αυτά που ακούω ("this makes me mad"), όπου φτωχός κι η μοίρα του ("when it rains, it pours"), τα χάλια μας ("look at our mess"), τα ριγμένα τα παιδιά ("oh, look at those wronged folks"), εγώ είμαι καμένος από αυτές τις ιστορίες ("I've learned my lesson"), especially when used by news hosts that are supposedly in the center of formality and ostensible respectability, really stand out.

Journalistic language is also known for its exaggerations and its lack of justifications, and this has been studied in Greek academia (Valiouli 2001; Diamantakou 2001). The expression of unjustified assessments makes it easier for emotions to be mobilized. The domination of emotion over reason, however, may block the recipients from being able to make logical or meaningful connections in order to further process the messages they receive. In other words, there is a possibility that the receiver may not even think about challenging what is supposedly obvious and self-evident. It is true, nonetheless, that the element of emotion is included in the private and domestic sphere, which is the purview of drama and, on a first level, it is peculiar to see it included in the respectable product of news broadcasts and political shows, which belong to the public, administrative, and relatively impersonal sphere.

Here, I believe it would be useful to mention words or phrases that have entered the Greek vocabulary under circumstances describing stereotypes about nations or nationalities or that bring to memory the Greek nation's struggles, such as Ottoman rule (χαράτσι or "tax," φέσι or "debt," το χαβά τους οι Τούρκοι or "the Turks won't change their tune," τουρκική μπαμπεσιά or "Turkish infamy," all words and phrases containing words of Turkish origins); the Italian occupation (μπλόκα or "blockades") or the French influence (στο γύψο or "ice" and ρουφιάνοι or "ruffians").[23]

2.8.5 Choosing popular topics

The safekeeping of a media discourse that is familiar, friendly, and approachable to the recipients requires a sector that will choose topics that show the problems, the anxieties, and the achievements of as many individuals and social groups as possible. The community feels the need to be able to have a say in the topics chosen and to see its own issues and its own interests be part of the public sphere. My research showed that the topics that were presented with a more vernacularized language, either when reported or commented on, were mostly about unemployment, high prices, farmer mobilizations, adult criminality, the people's view of the government, and the abandonment of the countryside.

What I observed was that the use of vernacular words or phrases, even their variations from different dialects, and also the use of neologisms and other idiosyncratic words was not only limited to "heavy" topics. While one would expect the findings to point to a preference for a vernacularized language about the problems of the weak socioeconomic classes or about spicy stories,

---

[23] From my findings, I will discuss just one example from an evening news broadcast: Τεφτέρια, βερεσέ και τα ταμεία στενάζουν. Δεν είναι άλλωστε λίγες οι φορές που το βερεσέ γίνεται φέσι και ο πελάτης καπνός. ("Buying on credit, but the registers suffer. Sometimes credit becomes debt and the customer disappears"). The word φέσι, which comes from the Turkish word fes, which refers to the usually red head cover Muslim people wear (Dictionary of Standard Greek 2001:1421), is used metaphorically to express an unpaid debt. Its use, combined with the use of the formal and ancient Greek verb στενάζω (to suffer) that is used mostly in contexts such as "For four hundred years, the Greek people suffered under the Turkish yoke" cannot be by accident. The two choices have complementary meanings due to their intertextual relation (Koutsoulelou-Michou 1997), and their goal is to express more powerfully the emotions of rage regarding the poverty of a group of citizens, maybe even a concealed anti-authoritative attitude.

I found, however, that there are no such constraints. Even in cases where the agents of media discourse dealt with truly serious issues, like corruption allegations within the justice system or the clergy being in crisis, the vernacularized language was always present.

2.9 Data Drawn on Media Metalanguage

2.9.1 The vernacular in television discourse

The journalists working at national TV stations who agreed to be interviewed for the needs of my research regarding the media during the first decade of the millennium agreed, more or less, that the language used on TV news and political shows by journalists has taken a turn to the vernacular. The reasons for such a turn were the following:

1. Media discourse took a parallel course to the overall evolution of the language, from its rigid and formal archaic form to the more popular demotic form.

2. The Greek media were influenced by foreign ones and followed the American standards specifically, where a less rigid and formal language started being used in comparison to how language was used in Greece in the decades before and after 1974.

3. It reflects the media attempt to further approach the greater mass of TV viewers for the past four decades. Television discourse addresses all the social strata, which have different education levels and experiences. Two processes helped with that goal. First, the increase in live broadcasts required fast and direct description of an event, which means that a simpler and more approachable oral speech was used. Second, news broadcasts were now presented by many people having conversations, which led to the language of the hosts being harmonized to the so-called average.

4. The viewership factor, or the adjustment of speech, was based on the sample that the viewership measurement companies use and not on the total number of viewers. I observed that journalists shape their speech according to each sample.[24]

---

[24] The fact that mostly retired people constituted the core of viewers for many years was taken into consideration.

5. The competition among privately owned TV stations to attract the largest audience.

6. The choice of popular topics. Language adjusted to those particular topics.

7. The limited vocabulary used by some of the journalists that were working only on television and had never been employed in the printed press.

8. The nature of media discourse, which is sloganized, given the fact that everything that is said functions or needs to function as a "slogan."

In the opinions of the agents of media discourse, the goals served by a vernacularized language from the reconstitution of democracy onwards are the following:

1. The transmission of easily-understood messages to the television audience so they do not get bored, given the fact that a viewer may be doing something else while watching TV.

2. Making journalists appear as people who are friendly and familiar to the audience.

3. Charming public opinion and mainly the working class that may not trust journalists who seem distant (a global phenomenon).

4. Flattering the public, making it like or support a certain journalist or news host. There was also some skepticism about the genuineness of the adoption of codes that flatter the audience, whose qualitative characteristics are known to TV stations thanks to qualitative TV viewership measurements but also to the adjustment of journalistic language to the language repertoire of the working classes. Besides, TV viewers are known to be flattered when they feel that a representative of authority speaks their own language and thus believe that he or she "is one of them."

2.9.2 Media and political discourse as communicating vessels

Media and political discourses seem as if they've always been communicating vessels since they are discourses which are social, public, and transmitted by the representatives of authority. However, estimates by the representatives of the press on how media and politics interact and influence each other were varied, if not conflicting.

There were opinions that media discourse followed political discourse. A different viewpoint suggests that the Panhellenic Socialist Movement (known mostly by its acronym PASOK) stayed in power for so long[25] that the language used by the socialists and by younger politicians ended up influencing journalists, who hoped to prove that they were progressive and in favor of the people. There was also a relevant opinion that media discourse followed political discourse in how vernacularized it was so that it could seem supportive of the citizens' interests. Others stated that politicians and journalists competed over who would convince the people that they could represent them and express their interests in the most efficient way.

It has also been testified that it was the politicians that imitated the language of journalists, so they could be more appealing and familiar to the people. That came after the success of TV shows that used vernacularized language and popular topics, so politicians were essentially forced to use the language employed by journalists.[26]

Finally, it was expressed that both spaces—politics and journalism—were feeding off each other on the level of language. When politicians discovered the power of television, they made sure to speak the way people spoke even more often and journalists, keeping watch over them, developed the *convergence to the bottom*. The politicians made heavy use of a "popular" version of language to show their support to the people, and television made sure it showed the vernacularized language of politicians.

In my opinion, this development shows a spiral of mutual, stated, or implied competition for the public's acceptance even though their goals differ depending on the occasion and circumstances (winning votes, gaining viewers, manipulation, sustaining current power structures, etc.).

2.9.3 Fictive sympathy and the attempt to "merge with the audience"

I took the theory of fictive sympathy and highly illusive intimacy to agents of media discourse and occasional hosts of evening news broadcasts and political shows on Greek television (Maria Houkli, Nikos Evangelatos, Michalis Kapsis,

---

[25] In government in the years: 1981–1989, 1993–1996, 1996–2004, and 2009–2011.

[26] A significant role was played by some magazines, including KLIK, whose editor-in-chief was Petros Kostopoulos. He exerted great influence and founded a school followed by certain politicians.

Konstantinos Arvanitis, Fotini Pipili, Maria Spyraki and others). They confirmed the general point of view, offering their own insights as well such as:

- The center of gravity of the news has been moved to a point where journalists now function as facilitators of the citizens' pain[27] and, instead of finding themselves in opposition to authority, they "converse" with it so they can make it easier for citizens to communicate with authority and solve their problems, though not always in a lawful way.

- A new order was developed in the news field in which various journalists and hosts have become managers of the citizens' pain[28] as well as negotiators, even though that is not their role.

- There was an attempt by journalists to charm public opinion, especially that of the working classes, an attitude that can be attributed to the influence of American standards on Greek media discourse (this is a global and not solely a Greek phenomenon).

- There was also the phenomenon of flattering the audience. One of the terms used was merging with the audience, which is something that requires a closer look; it integrates and absorbs various attempts at intimacy towards the audience and its goal is to utilize it to serve the interests of hierarchies.

Interesting, not only on a linguistic level but also on socioeconomic and political levels, were the answers I received on the question of whether friendliness and intimacy that was being sent out by media discourse after the reconstitution of democracy intended to suppress a) the closed nature and rigid organization of the medium and b) the fact that interests served by the medium were those belonging to its owners, whether visible and publicized, or concealed and mediated. From the varied and different answers given by the interviewed journalists, I surmised the following, depending on the case:

- Acceptance that the phenomenon is real but with the caveat that it applied mostly to journalists that work for the private TV stations and

---

[27] See also Tsitsanoudis-Mallidis 2012a.

[28] On the back cover of the volume of essays I edited titled Η διαχείριση του πόνου στη δημόσια σφαίρα. Από τη νηπιακή ηλικία έως την ενηλικίωση [Pain Management in the Public Sphere: From Infancy to Adulthood] (2012b), I claim that the phenomenon of dealing with pain gradually entered advertising discourse, social media, and the blogosphere. It surpassed politics and the media in their traditional forms. The dominance of hypermedia reduced the popularity of television at the same time that cellphones and tablet computers gave immediate access to alternative news and social media. The merciful and skillful management of human pain in the public sphere disposed of the inability to communicate pain and bloomed thanks to the attitude of illusive intimacy that was held by the guardians of pain towards those who suffer.

less to the ones working for the state TV, which was later called public,[29] where diverging from the "line, whether politically or economically" can cost journalists their job. No matter how rigid the organization of the medium is, its discourse can be vernacularized and emotional, and the journalists can sometimes appear as harsh and stern and sometimes as sympathetic members of the people so that they can overcome the difficulty of actually expressing their opinion and conceal the organizational rigidity of the medium.

- Denial that the phenomenon is real, calling this kind of reasoning not at all nuanced and such opinions demonizing, conspiracy theories, ludicrous, and so on.

- Critical attitude about the way some of these media function these days in Greece and the position journalists have in them.

- Judging that professional journalists are responsible for that since they create the media's "culture" and "aesthetics."

The journalistic language of news broadcasts of state or public television was tangentially related to the present research and it would be interesting to focus on that in the future. The general opinion, however, is that in state or public television the discourse is more careful because there are larger expectations regarding its educational role. Therefore, there are usually no "empty" and bombastic phrases, such as the ones chosen just to attract the audience; there is not an intensely axiological or pluralistic discourse, no melodramatic style, no clichés, etc. but a more rigid and conservative framework. In the context of this book and only tangentially, I want to point out a few issues that should be dealt with more systematically in the future:

- emphasis on the educational role of public radio-television and on the cultivation of aesthetics

- the removal of dramatized media discourse with public television and radio leading this effort

- partial or full disconnection of discourse from the commercial aspects and popularity of media

- making sure to disseminate, save, and protect the Greek language.

---

[29] The difference between the terms *state* and *public* television is about the degree of a supposed participation of the people in how the medium is governed. The term *public* is chosen to imply a social, participatory, and broader character in the medium and to dispose of the negative connotations of statism and of the medium's close relationship to any given government.

2.10 Conclusions

In this chapter, I attempted to analyze a distinguished part of the use of language—the language of journalists—my focus being on television. My working hypothesis, based on the theoretical tools available to me, was that for the past few years, and especially since the introduction of private television, a new language has been used coming from journalists who, by influencing and being influenced by the vernacularized language of politicians, attempt to appear approachable and as popular as possible. This new language is adjusted to the language standards of its recipients/viewers. Through the words themselves and their form, and not necessarily on the level of meaning and substance, this language attempts to give the impression that it possesses popular elements, that it comes, in other words, from the people. It tries to appear as the creation of the people, which addresses them, and which is ultimately a genuine expression of its positions and interests. This attitude held by the agents of media discourse, which I call attitude of fictive sympathy or attitude of highly fictive/illusive intimacy, is served by and imprinted in a language that gives the representatives and agents of journalistic power the ability to claim, using certain words and phrases, that they belong to the people and that they are socially sensitive, thus acquiring traits and benefits that they would otherwise have to acquire not with the form but with the content of their words.

The bibliography I used offered certain points of view which generally support the fact that, in the society of mass media, the dissociation from the standard language decreases to the point where it disappears, mainly due to a social assessment that assigns prestige and superiority to those who speak the "standard" language. However, what I discovered through gathering material from evening news broadcasts; personal interviews with distinguished agents of media discourse; and a survey that was given to one hundred recipients of television discourse was that the media discourse of television from the reconstitution of democracy onwards, even though it is by nature public and formal, recruited, on occasion, low-language varieties in order to expand its influence on the mass of TV viewers; successfully complete, alongside providing its recipients with news and information, its propagandistic function and manufacture of consent, shaping the opinions, attitudes and, ultimately, the ideology of the public; and secure a wide commercial appeal as a product.

In order for the above to happen, discourse would have to:

   a. appear familiar and popular to its recipients;

   b. give the impression that it closes the distance separating the viewers/recipients from the powerful media that transmit it, given the fact that there is a worrying phenomenon where media ownership is concentrated in only a few business circles; and

c. manage at the same time to convince the mass of viewers that it does not represent the interests of its owners (whether these are the state or private businessmen) but of the recipients themselves, who were led to see in the medium and its discourse their own expectations and positions.

Considering the fact that media ownership is now an oligopoly, we can see the incredible informational, political, and propagandistic power the media possess since whatever ideological weight they have may be a result of their affiliation with economic and political agents that used and still use the media as vehicles to increase their influence. The persons/owners may change, but this phenomenon does not cease to exist.

Furthermore, I present the ways and practices in which the attitude of fictive sympathy is constituted, focusing on the level of language. These ways mainly include the selective use of horizontal and vertical language variations, the elevation of the private and emotional element to the public sphere that was once reserved for official purposes, the artful interweaving of public and private sphere, the convincing expression of an ideological alliance between the medium and the people's demands and expectations and, of course, the increase in popular topics in evening news broadcasts. I believe that the above practices in their popularized form managed to bring profits and other communicational and financial benefits mainly to the private media which reigned in the public sphere in the years after the reconstitution of democracy and until the memoranda and shaped particular lifestyles and opinions.

2.10.1 Codifying the impact to the audience

After codifying the influence and impact of the attitude of fictive sympathy on its recipients, I want to stress four points:

A. The flattering destigmatization of the use of "inferior" linguistic codes. Recipients are not stamped by an inferiority stigma; their language is destigmatized, and they are also possibly flattered when they notice that media make use of the same or a similar linguistic code as the one they use which, in the context of public and formal discourse, could as well be rejected as inferior or inadequate. Especially as far as the use of dialects is concerned, even if it is just selective, recipients feel that their familiar linguistic idioms are not condemned as inferior deviations from the national, official norm; on the contrary, they are highlighted through their appearance in the media. In this atmosphere, recipients receive more easily the promoted commodity/product of the news, while it is far from impossible that they are even more vulnerable in relation to the ideology or the hidden agenda that a certain media might serve.

B. The expression of trust and sympathy towards the media/journalist. Recipients possibly trust more easily the media and the journalist who takes a stance of fictive sympathy, perceiving them quite often as spokespersons for the popular problems and interests. Quite often, they come to media's assistance when they feel or realize that they have no other means of access to the powerful and the decision-makers. They evaluate journalists as capable of handling their problems with effectiveness by substituting the agents responsible for finding solutions, such as the public sector or other institutionalized bodies of an organized state. They recompense the journalists and the media who adopt such a stance by watching their shows and their program, offering increased viewership ratings, which is measured via various qualitative means and which, in turn, plays a crucial role in the allocation of advertising funds in an undoubtedly competitive market. In the case of the print media, newspapers saw an increase in their circulation.

C. The disorientation danger. Although, in theory, mass media contribute to individual self-determination and to the formation of collective identities, when media present a virtually classless society in which the right to information and to be able to critique is distributed equally between rich and poor, then there exists a danger not only to hinder the development of individual self-determination but to disorient people as well, offering them false expectations about their environment and the position that they (could) hold in it. The mediated television media texts, as primary hearths of entanglement between the private/personal and the public/impersonal, between the domestic/emotional and the common, often create the impression that the distance between the agents of power and the powerless is cancelled. The audience was in clear danger of disorientation every time journalists expressed a general ideological alliance with the audience, every time media discourse acquired supposed magical qualities, and every time the social, political, or other hierarchy was undermined by an insincere effort to redefine power relations between the agents of media discourse and their recipients.

D. The danger of an uncritical reading of television texts. Texts which are marginalized in a vernacular style sometimes pose a danger of trapping or numbing the viewers. The danger of critical deactivation is particularly relevant when the vernacular style is complemented by a selection of frivolous topics, when information is replaced by rhetorical hyperboles and the viewership-craving emphasis on bedazzlement and drama, or when information and analysis are replaced by the processing of the individual problems of each individual viewer in an effort by journalists to function as mediators between political authorities and the common people.

However, the most crucial question is whether the viewers gain in power by such an attitude on the part of the media—namely whether the coercive relations of power, which are developed and cultivated by the contemporary powerful media, could transform into viewers' empowerment or into what Cummins terms *collaborative creation of power* (Cummins 2002).

According to the results of my research, the manifestation of the fictive sympathy stance towards the viewers is not on its own enough in order for the recipients to feel empowered and able to bring about radical changes in their lives and the social status quo or to feel that that their identities are included. The attitude of fictive sympathy, even as a result of an extreme compliance of the journalist/media discourse producer to the expectations and demands of the common people, possibly offers a relative encouragement to the viewers, albeit of unknown duration, if not restricted to the few minutes of publicity necessary for the needs of a reportage or a TV show. Even if the viewers experience the responsiveness of the media or the journalists to the particular problem that they may face, or even if they manage to present to the public their needs and interests through the airing of a television show, they do not feel at all secure that this temporary relationship will ever evolve into a meaningful and durable relationship, a true empowerment of their identities, and that it will not be consumed as another popular topic which will later be redeemed by analogous advertisement revenues.

2.10.2 Improving the language level

Undoubtedly, the viewers are heavily influenced by media discourse due to its wide dissemination in an era of spectacular expansion of the level of imposition of electronic media on large social strata, even if their role has decreased due to the intensive usage of social media. The educational role of media discourse and mass media in general, as well as the instructive influence on the recipients' language sense, could be commonly accepted, but this is not the case. Besides, the educational role of mass media does not constitute the top priority, especially among private television stations, where chasing viewership rates and unbounded competition are the rule.

Actually, within the framework of "opening up" the media to people of a lower social strata, it can be observed that the linguistic code chosen each time to be used in the various high-prestige television products such as news bulletins and news television shows, is not expanded since the richness of Greek language and its subsequent stylistic possibilities are not deployed. The reason behind this observation is assigned to the media's goal for the end product to be quickly and easily comprehended and consumed, to be free from the danger of becoming boring, and to protect the people's already held perceptions of the world.

Furthermore, there is an extensive compliance of media discourse with the linguistic codes of particular social groups, such as the elderly, who constituted for a large period of time the main portion of viewership in Greece. A compliance of this kind is based on particular stereotypical conceptions and expectations for the communicational needs and weaknesses of elderly people. Of course, we cannot exclude the fact that the use of a limited vocabulary was not due to intentional planning but a result of the poor vocabulary many journalists possessed.

The factors described above lead to the use of a restricted linguistic code, which consists of mainly descriptive notions, seeks refuge in hyperbole, risks the exhaustion of the meaning of words due to extensive dramatization, and ultimately exploits only a small part of the structural possibilities of language, avoiding their intensive and systematic deployment.

PART III

THE (POST-)MEMORANDUM LANGUAGE

3

The Language of Authority
in the Days of MoUs

3.1 Introductory Remarks

THE FUNCTIONS OF MEDIA DISCOURSE, in relation to the representation of the financial crisis and its consequences from the beginning of the implementation of the memorandum of understanding, have been studied this past decade both at intralinguistic and interlinguistic levels. The scientists involved in this study proceeded slowly and cautiously regarding its objectives. In the framework of my published research,[1] I addressed the memoranda texts on the internet and in print or electronic media early,[2] foreseeing that there would be a gradual new memorandum or post-memorandum language or neo-language (Fitoussi 2021)[3] which would be violently imposed from the top down.[4] Among the issues that were included in my approach were, on the one hand, the types of *discourses* chosen and their respective representations and, on the other hand, the primary language functions that were used, such as the descriptive and the expressive functions. During the analysis of the data, I examined on the level of form the verbal and nominal structures while, on a vocabulary level, I examined the use of words and phrases taken from the so-called vernacular or

---

[1] This chapter includes an enriched and partially revised version of my 2013 paper "Χαρακτηριστικά του δημόσιου λόγου σε απεικονίσεις της οικονομικής κρίσης στην Ελλάδα" [Public discourse characteristics in representations of the financial crisis in Greece] (see Section A of the Bibliography). The author would like to thank the editors of the journal for their permission to use the paper. The findings of this chapter were presented in my lecture, as a Fellow of Comparative Studies, at the Harvard Summer School in Olympia that was organized by Harvard University in Ancient Olympia in 2014. I would also like to thank Dr. Nicolas Prevelakis for his trust and encouragement when I was still pursuing this topic at a very early stage.

[2] See also my book *Language and Greek Crisis: An Analysis of Form and Content* (2013) in Section B of the Bibliography.

[3] See also the Bibliography, Section C for a link to a YouTube video of a discussion I participated in on Greek television on the topic of "Η νεογλώσσα του μνημονίου" [The neo-language of the memorandum].

[4] See also Tsitsanoudis-Mallidis 2011 in Section A of the Bibliography.

vernacularized language but also from the systematic or educated one. Finally, on a semantic level, I attempted to reveal the ways the ideological functions of the language are achieved, such as the authoritative and the propagandistic function, in an age of heavy propaganda in which consent is imposed and the language of fear is constantly used.[5]

3.2 Theoretical Framework and Method of Analysis

The study of the consequences of the financial crisis on modern Greek was focused on the various structural schemas and types of verbs used as well as the nouns that were found and indexed from a specialized and relatively homogeneous body of texts. Those were published texts in the traditional print and electronic media but also texts posted online in various blogs and news websites. These texts can all be considered journalistic both in the narrow and the wider sense of the term that points to a type of alternative and cooperative journalism. These texts came from the following data pools:

- published speeches by politicians in newspapers and magazines
- weekly and daily newspaper titles
- excerpts of analysis and other articles by online journalists

More specifically, these were 112 published texts with 258,289 words in total. I started amassing and indexing this textual evidence on February 22, 2011, and I completed it on March 26.[6] I chose discourse items that were produced naturally and spontaneously. I used a deductive approach which moved the genuine and unaltered data to theoretical processing.[7] Furthermore, I chose this particular composition of the corpus because it was necessary to examine the structure, the form, and the functions of the language that was transmitted by different transmitters, whether they were created by media organizations (and particularly television) or by political authority or by agents and people that did not belong to the publishing and political elite but worked within a framework of

---

[5] During the same time, I supervised a doctoral dissertation at the University of Ioannina undertaken by Mr. E. Theodoropoulos that was on the language of fear. I also organized the Second International Summer University on Greek Language, Culture and Media in collaboration with Harvard University's Center for Hellenic Studies in Greece which had the more specific title "The Language of Authority in the Days of the Memorandum." See also 4.4.

[6] Greece was entering some very harsh economic times and the low- and middle-income earners were facing major difficulties due to the financial measures that shrank their income and were coming one after another.

[7] This corpus does not include advertising texts nor texts from cartoons or satirical pieces since I believe that including them would expand the study to a point that would confuse the discussion on the data as well as the final conclusions.

"cooperative and alternative journalism."[8] My research approach was based on the fundamental principles of critical discourse analysis (Fairclough 2003).

3.3 Working Hypothesis

My study started with the working hypothesis that the experience of acceptance of the consequences of the financial crisis is probably depicted by and, at the same time, characterizes the various linguistic realities pertaining to public and private discourse. Since the citizens–"victims" are directly involved in the painful experience of the crisis, its influence—mostly negative—as well as various problems that have been created will appear in the vocabulary through structural schemas and verbal types but also through nominal phrases with the use of nouns, adjectives, and other phrases. Also, by considering the position that language is vernacularized by the choice of various language codes from the communication repertoire (Kostoula-Makraki 2001:54), and the view that high orality can be put into the service of an attitude of illusive sympathy (Tsitsanoudis-Mallidis 2011:133–135) that the agents of political or media public discourse wish to show to the mass of recipients, I formulated a second hypothesis regarding the description of the financial crisis. This hypothesis argued that in media and politics some elements of the vernacular are used consciously and cunningly in order to depict the huge consequences of the recession on the lower and middle classes more accurately. For example, as far as the public sphere is concerned, it was interesting to examine the *private language argument* (Wittgenstein 1989) given the fact that informal private language provides the opportunity to express facts, experiences, and situations with word schemas that are familiar to their recipients and whose use is congruent with their microcosm.

3.4 Linguistic Actualization: Categorizations and Examples

More specifically, I noticed that in the published texts that describe or denounce the recession and the memorandum, what was used was:

- vernacular phrases and words, which I put into two categories: verbal and nominal types
- common metaphors

---

[8] Regarding the significance of individualized and limited corpora of language data based on style, discourse field, and content, see De Beaugrande 2001:3.

- homonymous wordings–cliché words and phrases
- vulgar words and taboo phrases
- words and phrases from social dialects
- neologisms

Moreover, I observed an intensive use of private speech as opposed to the use of complex and "aristocratic" words that point to a "systematic" or "educated" language.[9]

3.5 Discussion of Latest Data

3.5.1 Verbal and nominal structures

Intransitive structures were used to denote unavoidable misfortunes, irreversible disasters, or tradition against the adversity of the situation. The crisis was depicted as a phenomenon that attacks horizontally and worsens an already existing situation. For instance: Σβήνει η Ελλάδα (Greece is being wiped away), Αργοπεθαίνει το έθνος (Greece is slowly dying), Η κοινωνία έπιασε πάτο (Society has hit rock bottom), Η χώρα βρίσκεται σε πόλεμο (The country is at war), Η σφαλιάρα πάει σύννεφο (We keep getting knocked down), etc.

Furthermore, intransitive types such as πεθαίνω (dying), αργοπεθαίνω (slowly dying), and φοβάμαι (fearing) were used to carry a semantic load whose size could better express primitive feelings and reactions but could also refer to the childhood of the sufferers (De Bleser and Kauschke 2003).

Conversely, transitive structures were used to express the provocative nature of the ambusher, the sudden attacks against the vulnerable but also the enraged demand of the wronged for the restoration of justice: for instance, Τώρα μπορείτε να χρεοκοπήσετε (Now you can go bankrupt), Η Μέρκελ κουρέλιασε το Γιώργο (Merkel destroyed Georgios), Φέρτε πίσω τα κλεμμένα! (Bring back what was stolen!). In most of these verbal structures, the effects of the financial crisis are depicted holistically, as if they had permeated the entire Greek society and not just one of its parts, for example: Σέρνεται η ελληνική κοινωνία (Greek society limps along) and Η κοινωνία αγκομαχάει (Society gasps for air).

It was observed that in the case of transitive as well as the case of intransitive verbal structures, the verbs were delivered simultaneously or alternately with exclamations, which supports the view that there is a parallel exclamatory function in the sufferer's discourse or the discourse of those who describe the crisis.

---

[9]   For more about systematic language, see also 3.5.5.

I also detected cases where the recession and the memoranda were becoming, both in syntax and meaning, the subject of intransitive verbs such as Η κρίση βαθαίνει (The crisis deepens). I interpreted this phenomenon as a linguistic element that depicts the crisis as an unbidden and generally living entity[10] with the traits of an undesired and revolting guest in a once delimited and possibly protected space, which of course reflects the interests and views of the lower and middle classes.[11]

With the use of nominal structures, the effects of the crisis as well as the crisis itself were realized as a threatening entity separate from yet connected to society. Nouns such as μαχαίρι (knife), θηλιά (noose), τσεκούρι (axe), καταιγίδα (storm), and πείνα (hunger) are stereotypically found in published texts. These structures were useful insofar as they could transmit such messages in an easily understood form. Especially as far as knife, noose, and axe are concerned, the representation of the effect would be accompanied by the tool or object itself, so there would be a reference to a *knife* and not to *cutting*, to a *noose* and not to *suffocation*. In other words, the representation was based on a metonymic relation, i.e. the object/means and not the action/result of its use. This use of vivid descriptive nouns led to a very representational description of the effects of the crisis.

Further verbal and grammar data analysis led me to the conclusion that the recession and the memoranda were perceived as unfortunate developments from which citizens wanted to be released in any way possible, no matter how unfeasible that was, as depicted in phrases such as ανοχύρωτοι (unfortified), ανυπεράσπιστοι (defenseless), and αφοπλισμένοι οι εργαζόμενοι (the workers are disarmed), etc.

It goes without saying that the depiction of the recession and the crisis differed each time in the traits that were attributed to them, their aggressiveness, or their intensity. Among the adjectives used to represent intensity, one

---

[10] Here, I would like to thank Dr. Chryssoula Lascaratou, Professor Emerita of Linguistics at the National and Kapodistrian University of Athens, for the help, feedback, and inspiration I received from her while studying social pain in the media in today's age of financial crisis. Her works on the function of language in the experience of pain and, more specifically, the use of metaphor in its structures and depictions influenced my way of thinking and led me to new avenues of research. I also had the honor of including one of her essays in the essay collection I edited titled *Η διαχείριση του πόνου στη δημόσια σφαίρα. Από την παιδική ηλικία έως την ενηλικίωση.* [Pain management in the public sphere. From childhood to adulthood]. See also Lascaratou 2012.

[11] It would be very interesting to see these in the context of human pain and its language (see Lascaratou and Marmaridou 2005 and Lascaratou 2008). Pain becomes a perpetrator, and its personification becomes possible by "promoting" pain to a subject of transitive verbs like χτυπώ (hit), ταράζω (disturb), τινάζω (shake), πνίγω (choke), σφίγγω (tighten), σφάζω (butcher). According to Lascaratou (2008), this way pain acquires the characteristics of a living entity and is depicted on the semantic level as an evil enemy who attacks and tortures the sufferer.

would see the following: δυνατός (strong), σκληρός (tough), αφόρητος (unbearable), αβάσταχτος (unbearable), αντιλαϊκός (anti-popular) etc. Most frequently used was the loaded adjective σκληρός (tough), followed by αδυσώπητος (ruthless) and ανελέητος (merciless). The situation was described with an emphasis on the victims of the economic recession, who were described as τρομαγμένοι (scared) and, metaphorically, as πελαγωμένοι (lost at sea) and βρεγμένοι (bedraggled). Finally, taboo language was frequently used (Allan and Burridge 2006) with a parallel use of pronouns such as εμείς οι μαλάκες (us suckers) and [οι άλλοι] οι νταβατζήδες (those pimps) etc. These schemas offer a contrasting or a conflicting—perhaps even arbitrary—delimitation between a general we/us (that is, the people) and the others (those in power, the lenders, or the institutions). *We* became synonymous with "victim" while the *others* were deemed as those responsible for the situation *we* have found ourselves in.

3.5.2 Metaphorical representations

The observed use of metaphorical discourse in the depictions of the dimensions and effects of the financial crisis confirms the theory that the metaphor is an integral part of the communication of ideas and experiences that we would otherwise have trouble expressing in monosemic terms (Deignan 2005:133). In this case, the use of metaphorical discourse was strongly associated with the intention to facilitate the meaningful transmission and explanation of the effects of the crisis on the working classes mainly. Clarity regarding the description of the effects was achieved through metaphor, in ways that made it possible for the recipients of the text to quickly recognize the painful experience they were directly, and painfully, involved in.[12]

Metaphorical words such as *knife*, *noose*, or *axe* depicted the effects of the crisis in a dramatic fashion, a crisis that became a fatal threat, an invasion. There are similar representations in descriptions of chronic illnesses or pain (Sontag 1991; Gwyn 1999; Semino, Heywood and Short 2004). It is worth adding that the various characteristics of the crisis are often depicted through the mechanism of metonymy, allegory, or reflection. The effort to inform about the serious dimensions and effects of the financial crisis on society led the designers and authors of texts to choose structured descriptive terms whose reference points were common metaphors and similes, for example: ναυάγιο εσόδων (revenue shipwreck) or Το μουλάρι το βγάζει από τη λάσπη ο αγωγιάτης (It's the mule driver who gets his mule out of the mud), a common expression in Greek meaning that the leaders are responsible for fixing problems. Quite often they would choose loaded and intertextually laden words and phrases like Πάμε μαζί στο χορό του

---

[12] For more about the language of pain and its metaphors, see also Papadopoulou–Mantadaki 2019.

Ζαλόγγου (We are all dancing the dance of death) or Μας κουρελιάζουν (They left us in tatters).

Generally speaking, metaphors and similes used in the linguistic representations of the effects of the memoranda and the financial recession managed to show that the crisis was a self-existent entity with intimidating characteristics.

More specifically, I observed that the metaphorical representations of the Greek debt, the country's financial state, and especially the decline in standards of living in Greece aimed not just for the expression of sympathy and solidarity towards the sufferers but for the creation of schemas that created not only victim blaming but also a mass substitution of the people. These processes would "shepherd" the people towards a coercive submission to the "remedies" imposed by financial institutions that claim to be better able to "save" the people.

Specific language uses attempted to turn—or facilitate the transformation of—the Greek bankruptcy from a financial issue of the state into a problem of the people, who were persuaded that they were exclusively responsible for the financial situation and had to suffer the repercussions of their choices and failures in the recent past and the present.[13]

The financial crisis was depicted as a disease that the debtors, i.e. the people, suffered from and would not be cured of if they did not adopt the medical advice proposed by the perceived "doctors."[14] This schema was simple and abstract, and was based on a simple distribution of roles and schemas anchored in primal human fears. It was the following:

debt = disease

bankrupt Greek society = patient

lenders, institutions = doctor

financial measures = medicine, treatment

This analogy was made using words familiar to the masses, taken from a medical vocabulary. This vocabulary did not disturb the recipient's microcosm and, contrary to the financial measures that were depicted with a cryptic language, it included words that were quick and easy to understand. More specifically, the debt was depicted as a disease or condition that was not clearly or directly

---

[13] See also Gavriilidou 2017.

[14] Everything that follows in this section is a revision of my earlier study "Οι γιατροί και οι ασθενείς των μνημονίων" [The doctors and patients of the memoranda] that is included in the volume of collected essays that I edited titled *Ελληνική γλώσσα, πολιτισμός και ΜΜΕ* [Greek language, culture and mass media] (2017b).

defined but was thought to be serious and to lead to severe disabilities or sudden loss of life.

I observed some vagueness regarding the definition of the disease, despite the clear suggestions of its severity, as the afflicted organism was sickly and vulnerable, its deterioration was expected, and it could lead to certain or sudden death. The course of the disease was ill-omened and escalating. The causes of the disease were described as a vague type of genetic anomaly, disorder, serious injury, shock, depression, infection, and so on. The disease was often associated with pain in the extremities (hand or foot), something that could potentially require violent amputation by a doctor.[15]

This disease was defined through the depiction of its consequences. The patient could be described as wearing a cast,[16] as being in an intensive care unit, under sedation, in a coma, as wearing an oxygen mask, etc. The reference to oxygen evoked a necessary element of life and it formed an antithesis to the concept of asphyxia, which is a condition that is characterized by the breath slowing down or even stopping and that results in the body being deprived of oxygen. The use of this phrase generated a very unpleasant sense of claustrophobia or confinement, the patient being threatened by their pulse stopping, which would lead to the worst possible outcome. One of the direst consequences was, after all, sudden death.[17]

Sometimes there was a distinction made between the bankrupt Greek society and each individual citizen of Greece, other times there was not. In cases of generalization, the society as a whole was responsible for the state it had found itself in, with the metaphor of an epidemic or an infection being used to describe that state. The relapsing and unhealthy people were threatened by the worst possible outcomes, which were amputation, asphyxia, heavy disability, or even death. This vagueness regarding the type of disease was artfully and systematically cultivated, as the goal was to stir fears and reflexes that go all the way back to the first years of a person's life. Phrases were simple and direct so that they could simulate a child's automatic reactions. In multiple texts, the patients were all individual members of the community, which I thought was due to the fact that there was an effort to create individual responsibilities

---

[15] There are two characteristic examples of this use of language: "You need to choose: either you die, or they cut off your leg" and "When the hand is in pain, you don't cut it off." The people are in pain, and you *amputate* the country.

[16] The reference to wearing a cast is characterized as strongly *intertextual* since it points to older statements by the dictator Georgios Papadopoulos during the junta years (1967–1974): "I will attempt once more to come into contact with the doctors. We have a patient here; we will put him in a cast."

[17] Relevant examples include: "Bankruptcy will come as sudden death" and "The sudden death of the Greek economy."

regarding the actions and failures of each individual. The distinction was made so each member of the Greek society can bear the blame for everything that has happened. The individual was coerced into accepting a supposed—even biological—inferiority, in the context of a *cultural invasion* by those who are superior. Those who are inferior have no other option but to *normalize* this construct, to appropriate it, and to act according to their awareness of the dire situation they are in.

Structures with purely exclamatory function were also interesting, as the verbal depiction often contained exclamations.[18] On the other hand, the lenders were described as the *saviors* or *rescuers,* the doctors who are necessary and are the only ones who can save the patient from the disease, its effects, and possibly death.

Furthermore, during the years 2015–2016, a debate took place in the public sphere on the matter of whether lenders (δανειστές) should be called as such or whether we should start calling them "creditors" (πιστωτές) or even "institutions" (θεσμοί), which takes away the negative connotations of the lender and installs an institutional prestige and legitimacy on the agents that pressure Greece into repaying its loans with humiliating terms. It is a clear attempt to *manufacture consent* through language and its influential function.[19] The phenomenon of *renaming content*, as I call it, is of course not Greek and it is not only observed in politics[20] but also within the technology sector.[21]

The lenders were presented as having the characteristics of a savior, as they were ascribed the role of doctors who can give the patient the necessary drugs or treatment, even the most bitter of pills.[22] And while the texts did not specify the type of disease or condition and only insisted on how serious it was and how it could lead to death, they however emphasized the supposed expertise of the doctors, who required our trust and at the same time claimed how reliable and effective they were. The doctors were directly or indirectly depicted as experts, whose superiority could not be shaken or doubted. As a result, the sufferers had no choice but to be forced into total submission and adjustment to the orders of doctors whom they were not allowed to criticize or object to. There would be no reservations or doubts and, of course, no kind of claims contrary to what

---

[18] "My God! He won't make it!"
[19] See also Chomsky 1987.
[20] See also Denaxa 2019.
[21] See also the Bibliography, Section C for a link to an article in *Ta Nea* newspaper titled "Η τεχνολογία αλλάζει σταδιακά το νόημα των λέξεων που σχετίζονται με τη φύση" [Technology is gradually changing the meaning of words related to nature].
[22] "Don't fight the doctor" or "The doctor may give you drugs that you don't like, but even if you don't like them, the doctor is there to help."

the doctors ordered, for example: "You should do what the doctor ordered; he knows."

In my opinion, the language representations of the lenders as doctors that come to cure the alleged patients served a strategic "bipolar" perception, given that in order to impose a powerful healer, there first needs to be a helpless, desperate, and tragic creature like the patient that has been left vulnerable by nature and is limited by it. This schema is bloated, exaggerated, and underlines the following extremes:

- the helpless, desperate patient versus the powerful doctor
- tragedy versus eminence, imposition
- vulnerability, inferiority versus salvation, superiority

This apparent "symmetry" was created to serve a distorted, in its political correctness, yet strictly imposed representation that had adverse effects on the formation of images and perceptions of the responsibilities of citizens of a country that faced a financial crisis. The indebted citizens and their country had to buy into the *strategy of fear*, a narrative that capitalist systems of power employ internationally (Papadimitriou 2012).[23] Showing "facts" was intimidating and threatening, and the goal was to cause such distress in the recipients that they would accept this particular version of the crisis.

Finally, the harsh financial measures were considered the cure for the disease. The word διάσωση (rescue) was systematically used[24] and became oversized, dramatized, and exaggerated, which activated reflexes of a certain type in recipients. It was not by chance that the *inferior* or *low social varieties* (Mitsis 1999:31, 46, 90–91) that were used to depict the size of the problem or to blame the recipients were put up against an educated and systematic vocabulary.[25]

3.5.3 Quasi-literary, farcical, private language

The textual items of discourse that are being studied showed some nominal structures that are variations of literary passages, novel and poem titles, popular sayings, proverbs, and folk songs such as οι σύγχρονοι άθλιοι (the modern miserable) and οδός μνημονίου αριθμός μηδέν (memorandum street no. zero)

---

[23] The natural fear that people feel is gradually transformed into a *fear of authority*. Television, and the public sphere in general, functions as a metaphorical belt of deconstruction of social cohesion since the dramatization of events activates existing insecurities in people, and this results in the cultivation not of a collective conscience but of an unrestricted individualism. The activation of the citizens' inner fears makes them ideologically vulnerable, ready to accept every choice made by the political system.

[24] In the sense of averting danger or a disaster, often fatal.

[25] See 3.5.5.

etc. These structures were widely dialectal, intertextual, and were included in the microcosm of the recipients. They were mainly recruited in report titles, usually in a derisive or humorous way in order to mock reality. They are types of discourse that move between the literary and the theatrical and contain elements of artless lyricism and of a farcical language.

Besides, the limits between the vernacular and the vernacularized, as well as the literary and the poetic style can become unclear. As a result, the attempts to make a clear and evident distinction serve no purpose.

Just as in the case of metaphorical discourse, there is an intense emotional element in the use of private language. Further, language does not merely depict that world of emotions but can also structure and restructure it (Pavlenko 2002:209).

In the use of private language, I observed structures that had a clear exclamatory function, as the verbal representation was used simultaneously or alternately with typical or other interjections like Θεέ μου! Με πάνε για σφαγή! (My God! They are taking me to slaughter!). Those private expressive linguistic elements served as a direct and representational linguistic description of the effects of the financial crisis. They raised the scale of expressiveness and pointed to automatic natural reactions. This was merely a type of gradation of the emphatic function of private language.

3.5.4 Clichés, taboos, and lower social varieties

Plenty of the representations used to depict the crisis were not original but common, predictable, or even conventional in comparison to the widely used terms. For example, the use of the word *shock* was very frequent in titles and other texts that were studied for this research.[26] This frequent use served the need for a vivid depiction of the severity and the aggressiveness of the problems and the measures that were taken due to the memorandum. It was usually accompanied by exclamations and appropriate punctuation such as exclamation marks or exclamation marks with ellipses, thus confirming what has already been asserted in this book on the expression of the exclamatory function. Of course, the systematic and excessive use of intensely-loaded stereotypical words and phrases makes them run the risk of losing their meaning.

Another observation of mine was the clear use of taboos. These are words that carry negative allusions to sex, e.g. Το ΔΝΤ καρφώνει την Ελλάδα (The IMF nails Greece), or to a person's natural functions e.g. σκατά (shit) and also swear

---

[26] This particular word has been a cliché in media discourse ever since the reconstitution of democracy.

words and vulgarities like μαλάκες (suckers) and νταβατζήδες (pimps).[27] The use of vulgar words or more general taboo words helped the transmitters intentionally include some anti-authoritarianism in their speech and express some kind of revolt and reaction against the choices of the elites that repress the people.[28] This is a discourse that borders on the vulgar, as one can easily see in the use of negatively stigmatized words and phrases.

There were also some elements of a vernacularized style with the use of words that belong to the so-called slang or the dialect of the dispossessed. The use of such structures, either verbal or nominal, by the producers and the agents of discourse was ironic, derisive, and denouncing. Their goal was to rail against the poor state of Greece and the effects of the financial crisis and recession and/or to show who the ones supposedly responsible for such a negative situation are.

Every time the consequences of the financial crisis were described, there was also an accompanying preference for words and phrases that belonged to the oral, informal language, the dialects of the working classes or the young. The use of known words as slogans which imitate the vernacular style was frequent, for example: πλιάτσικο (pillage), χλαπάτσα (gunk), and μπίχλα (filth).[29]

Furthermore, there were words and phrases widely dialectal but known in urban centers and with great geographic and social distribution. As the positive simultaneous use of the vernacular or a vernacularized language (Fragkoudaki 1999:210) was also utilized, the producers of discourse and the authors of texts attempted to give the impression that they are ideologically allied with and supporters of the social classes, especially the lower ones, which were most afflicted by the crisis.

However, I believe that these uses functioned as "corruptions" of the typical and official language and, on the level of meaning and content, as an indirect and cryptic promise for less abstract and repressive texts, for an unleashing of criticism against public discourse, and for a revolt against the dominant class and the associations it has imposed (Tsitsanoudis-Mallidis 2006:184).

---

[27] Triantafyllidis (1963:72) claims that to characterize a word as χυδαία (vulgar) meant that it had a foreign etymology, and it was assessed on a social and not a linguistic basis. "Vulgar" are the words that are mostly used by the common people and are "avoided by the upper classes." This assessment however can also work in reverse; for example, the upper classes prefer the word κουζίνα (kitchen) and not the more vulgar Greek word μαγερειό (which is a synonym of kitchen). See also Fragkoudaki 1999:79.

[28] The word *people* here has romantic connotations.

[29] The various types of style are taken from the *Dictionary of Standard Greek* 2001.

3.5.5 The opposite systematic/refined language

On the opposite side of base or low social varieties, there was a use of beautiful and aristocratic words that were exploited or, to avoid loaded expressions, utilized by the agents of political, economic, and media propaganda.[30] For example, words such as αποπληρωμή (repayment), επιμήκυνση (prolongation), αναδιαπραγμάτευση (renegotiation), αναδιάρθρωση (restructuring), εκσυγχρονισμός (modernization), αναδιάταξη (recomposition), εξυγίανση (reforming), επανατοποθέτηση (reinstating), επικαιροποίηση (updating), επανεκκίνηση (restarting), and αναζωογόνηση (revivification) are just some examples of nouns that were frequently used by politicians and the media to depict not exactly the effects of the crisis but the appropriate and "correct" moves aimed at ending the crisis and recession.

Elaborate and respectable words became the representation of well-designed solutions that solve the problem, and these words became mainstream. The attempted creation of realities through language and especially through respectable words had and still has one goal: with its recipient being an audience of masses and not of individuals, it wanted to deconstruct the "actual reality" and create a new fictive and illusive reality whose protagonists would be those who wanted to convince the people that they are allied with them and have only their interests in mind.

3.6 The Child in Post-memorandum Texts: An Unexplored Field

The phenomenon of dealing with cases of pain as it was diffused through time by media and advertising discourse as well as in social media and blogs went beyond politics and mass media in their traditional forms. Infancy and childhood were no exceptions. In extreme cases, children became instruments of discourse like goods waiting to be exchanged.[31] The textual-linguistic and psycholinguistic

---

[30] Papanoutsos (2008) writes about how words decay and mentions "vulgarities and decline." He notes that "the decay of words is telling lies and falsifying not by accident but on purpose by those who use them. Then words lose their virtue. They provoke, they enrage with their false glamour, their fraudulent beautification. They stop being sincere... The nobler the words, the bigger the danger of their humiliation because of bad usage. The common, vulgar words face no such danger. However, those whose origins are noble are easier to debase and it happens very often especially if their meaning is respectful..." He mentions the words συμμαχία (alliance) and δημοκρατία (democracy) as characteristic examples of such misuse. This passage can be found in his essay titled "Η φθορά των λέξεων–Το δίκαιο της στιγμής" [The decay of words: The right of the moment].

[31] See also the Bibliography, Section C for a link to a summary of a paper I presented with E. Theodoropoulos titled "Η τηλεοπτική διεκπεραίωση του πόνου. Η θέση των παιδιών στη δημόσια

study of child management by journalists and advertisers during the crisis and the memoranda is a serious research challenge. Journalists and advertisers were then creating a social reality through journalistic texts which targeted the children's families and relatives as recipients.

Children and toddlers in post-memorandum advertising were never ignorant of what was happening in their families and the adult world in general. They were depicted as personalities that know, understand, and are affected by the serious consequences of the economic crisis. Their participation in advertising texts through monologues or dialogues served the attempts of the designers of advertising discourse to show the size of the effect the recession had on them, to emotionally manipulate the consumer, and to show how effective the product sold is since its purchase would work as a "magic wand" that could be used to take all childhood problems away. The descriptions of children's views on what happened in their microcosm used a simple language that appropriated elements of baby talk (Ferguson 1964:103-114). It was an adjustment to the child-as-interlocutor's code that is supposed to have diminished language skills.

Finally, the descriptions of the children's views and positions about the situation at home, which influences their relationship with their parents, are expressed using a simple language that sometimes tends to appropriate elements of baby talk. It is an expected adjustment by the recipients of advertising discourse to the child-as-interlocutor's code that is supposed to have weak language skills. This tendency to simplify speech and to adjust to the interlocutor's limited language skills leads to a certain type of baby talk, given the fact that it characterizes almost every speaker that addresses babies or toddlers. It can also be included in the cases of *downward convergence* of speech, in which a person with greater prestige or a higher level of language skills talks to someone who has just started to learn the language or is unable to enrich it.[32]

I tried to discuss these issues with my students while teaching in the postgraduate program of the Pedagogy Department for Kindergarten Teachers at the University of Ioannina, and their participation and response was very positive.[33]

σφαίρα" [The televisual processing of pain. The position of children in the public sphere] and to an additional paper I presented at the same conference titled "Γλωσσικές απεικονίσεις των παιδιών και των νηπίων σε ελληνικές μεταμνημονιακές διαφημίσεις" [Linguistic depictions of children and toddlers in Greek post-memorandum advertising].

[32] For more details, see the Bibliography, Section C for a link to a PDF of my paper titled "Οι γλωσσικές απεικονίσεις της οικονομικής κρίσης στον ελληνικό διαφημιστικό λόγο - Ενδεικτικές αναπαραστάσεις σημερινών νηπίων και παιδιών" [Linguistic representations of the financial crisis in Greek advertising discourse - Examples of child and toddler representations.]

[33] The course was "Language representations of infancy in the financial crisis"; the postgraduate program of the Pedagogy Department for Kindergarten Teachers was called "Preschool Education"; and the unit was "Language representations of children in post-memorandum advertising," which was a part of "Seminar I: Cross-sectional Seminar" in the same program.

3.7 Conclusions

In this chapter, I address the linguistic structures that were employed to describe the economic crisis in Greece and its consequences, especially after the implementation of the so-called memorandum beginning in May 2010. In order to conduct an analysis of discursive representations, I studied texts published in traditional and conventional mass media as well as on the internet.

It can be observed that the representations of situations and feelings faced by the patients of the crisis were constructed via a variety of structures, mainly noun and verb phrases. With verb phrases, speakers usually expressed the sufferers' deep involvement in the crisis predicament, while noun phrases were mainly characterized by their descriptive function. Verb phrases created a sense of something that was in progress while noun phrases served to create a sense of distance and completion in relation to the situations and feelings to which they referred.

The people were depicted as deeply involved in the painful experience of being "victims," a characteristic which in turn informed the overall style and form of linguistic actualization. The depiction of the consequences of the economic crisis via verbal constructions suggests that the designers and producers of public discourse preferred an active, direct, and dynamic representation of the crisis and its negative consequences. The use of nominals, on the other hand, and especially of adjectival modifiers, served to create the impression that people handle the problems that arise from the crisis in a passive manner with no available possibilities for escape or reaction.

Both constructions lexicalize the consequences of the MoUs in a way which enhances the dramatization of the produced discourse, as it also results by the use of stigmatized nouns and verbs. As far as the verbal constructions are concerned, the meanings of intransitive constructions are distinguished from those of transitive constructions, highlighting the holistic representation of the crisis as a substance diffused throughout the totality of Greek society and especially the low and middle social strata.

The lexico-grammatical analysis of the data offered the conclusion that the consequences of the crisis and the crisis itself were linguistically actualized as an independent, personalized, and objective existence, although connected to society. Another pervasive discursive strategy was the use of metaphorical language for the representation of the economic impasse, especially for these cases where technical terms or certain concepts of the macro-level could not be easily understood by lay people if expressed in literal or synonymic terms. The indebted people were presented as "patients," often characterized by primitive reactions of despair. Furthermore, we noted the introduction of elements typical in literary discourse or even humoristic and absurdist discourse, as well as elements from the discourse of the private sphere of which the prominence of affective language is a typical characteristic. The moderate use of taboo words and vulgar vocabulary was also not absent. In these choices, one can diagnose an anti-establishment attitude and a tendency to doubt the choices of the elites at the expense of the people.

As far as the linguistic varieties are concerned, I dealt mainly with vertical differentiations (social dialects) and secondarily with geographical variations. The result of this research showed that in order for the consequences of the economic crisis to be depicted, *low-prestige* social varieties were mainly used with clear characteristics of popular elements in discourse. The observed usage of vernacular words and phrases, either to an excessive degree or only occasionally, alongside the appearance of non-narrative elements mixed with the narrative, lead me to the conclusion that the producers and designers of media discourse of this style and kind desire to render themselves familiar and accessible to their audience.

While vernacular language was used since the reconstitution of democracy bearing the connotations of progressiveness and social sensitivity, the same usage is accompanied by different intentions in the era of MoUs, namely to assign blame to the citizens ("We ate it together," was a famous phrase uttered by Theodoros Pangalos[34] which meant that the political establishment and citizens "ate" [i.e. wasted] state money in cahoots with each other) and to incriminate and stigmatize them for the economic predicament in which Greece found itself ("You Greeks did a shitty job"). Vernacular and popular language, which was deployed in the framework of the fictive sympathy stance and cultivation of an illusive intimacy/closeness or in service of the "opening up" and the intrusion of political and media discourse into lower social strata, for either ideological or commercial reasons, is now employed in order to construct a narrative that resembles an indictment and to stigmatize individuals who, as massified elements, have no other choice but to accept an "inferiority" in relation to an alleged cultural, social, and economic "superiority" of the capitalists.

It is suggested that the expression of ideological alignment, which constituted the motive for the adoption of vernacular style in the past, seems to collapse since media discourse has ceased to be supportive of the various powerless social groups and has become normative and suggestive.

At the antipode of vernacular variations, a cryptic, systemic, and cultivated language was employed using compound and "aristocratic" words that were

---

[34] Theodoros Pangalos is a Greek politician, former member of the parliament and minister, and leading member of the Panhellenic Socialist Movement (PASOK).

placed in the public discourse in order to beautify tyrannical measures dictated and supported by various, largely of unknown origin, economic and politico-publishing systems of power in the name of an escape from the crisis. The vehicle of this imposition was the use of pretentious words of a processed and superior code whose meanings, however, were transformed analogously to the intentions of the elites. The redefinition of meanings and concepts concerned dozens of words and was assimilated immediately, violently, and decisively by the publishing-television system. The plethora of semasiological changes, in the throes of a constantly dramatized media and political discourse, did not ask for the speech community's consent, but it was legitimized in a top-down fashion by the media. This is an impressive phenomenon which would be worthy of study by future researchers.

To be exact, there was very little time for this violent modification of contents to mature. There was the impression that the "troika" (the three institutions that oversaw the so-called bailout of Greece, i.e. the European Commission, the European Central Bank, and the International Monetary Fund) and the memoranda rewrote the Greek dictionaries and thesauri, ignoring and cancelling age-old meanings and contexts without any previous or subsequent negotiations. I can even say that aside from public opinion, it's the language itself that was manipulated since it went through the effort of testing the limits of its recipients' perceptions in order to serve a political and mainly financial hegemony.

PART IV

REINFORCING THE EDUCATIONAL ROLE OF THE MEDIA

A MODERN IMPERATIVE

4

Asserting the Educational Function and Aesthetics

4.1 Less Hegemonic Texts: Is It Possible?

4.1.1 Desire for absoluteness, or awareness of the relativity of power?

WHAT REMAINS a challenge in contemporary societies and within the framework of a constant effort towards a *caring* society is the transformation of coercive relationships into *cooperative* and *additive* ones, in which the journey into otherness and the navigation towards difference will not be restricted by preconceived results (Cummins 2002:280). Even if this is an almost utopian goal, it still is necessary to fight for.

As far as media discourse is concerned, I declare myself to belong among those who support the need for it to transform into a kind of discourse which will not be dominated by the desire for absoluteness and the one-and-only god-like mediated product but will be directed by the awareness of the relativity of power and the realization of the inadequacy of mediation (Chatzisavvidis 2000:73). I ponder on the prerequisite degree of durability of an ideal kind of media discourse which can accommodate (self)cancellation and (self)regulation like a reflection projected onto a distorted mirror which, in turn, is conceived by its recipients as distorted itself. How many reframings and (de)codifications or restructurings would be necessary for the constitution as well as for the observation of this reflection?

The awareness of the points that are open to interpretation in each discourse occurrence, in conjunction with their problematic and invisible nature, could contribute to the realization of the poverty and gaps in the alleged power of the journalistic language. Imperfections, deficiencies, flaws, and confusions never cease to be among the essential traits of a living language. Language is, after all, an imperfect system.

In times of such uncertainty and continuously evolving changes, focusing on the demand for less hegemonic and authoritative texts has to be connected to practices that will decrease chauvinism and racism. In 2016, as a member of the Local Expert Committee and a seminar instructor specializing in the language of the media in the Hellenic Broadcasting Corporation's European Respect Words program, I worked with a team whose goal was to spread best practices on how to deal with hate speech in European media.[1] We compiled a code of conduct in which we emphasized how journalists should cover issues such as immigration, ethnic and religious minorities, Muslim minorities, and the Jewish community. The first and most important practice we recommended was the careful use of language, pointing out that those who shape language ought to consider the ideologies and the associations behind the words. Other suggestions were to avoid exaggerations, oversimplifications, prejudice, and criminalization but also to include discourse in "acceptable narratives." We also pushed for more control and moderation regarding the uncritical reproduction of stereotypes so that it would become possible to build around issues in humane ways, issues that should not always be considered part of the "law and order" narrative. We also underlined the importance of not using the wrong terminology, of respecting the privacy of individuals, especially if they belong to disadvantaged groups, and so on (Respect Words 2018).

A second axis was the creation of an online interactive map of European best practices regarding the language of journalists and a third one was an extensive European radio campaign that would take place through news broadcasts, interviews, and messages that would spread awareness and understanding regarding the humanitarian crisis and its description.

These are practices that showcase a challenge against an obsession with absoluteness in communications and in the language of journalists, and it would be useful if they caught on and even improved in the immediate future if we want to at least work on decreasing the authoritative character of texts.

However, they only provide the cure for one side of the problem.

---

[1] The action was organized by the European Commission and, more specifically, by the Commissioner responsible for issues of justice and consumers as part of the European Rights, Equality and Citizenship Programme (2014-2020). The following organizations participated in the aforementioned program: Asociación De Emisoras Municipales y Comunitarias de Andalucía de Radio y Televisión (Andalusian branch of EMA/RTV in Spain), Comharchumann Cumarsaide Pobal Bhaile Atha Cliath-T. (Ireland), ERREPI S.p.A—RADIO POPOLARE (Italy), Radio Student Association-RADIO STUDENT (Slovenia), Foundation for Civil Radio Broadcasting (CIVIL RADIO) (Hungary), Radio Dreyeckland Betriebs GmbH (Germany), International Press Institute (Austria). See also the link to the Respect Words website in Section C of the Bibliography, Chapter 4, n1.

4.1.2 The passion of ignorance

Communication cannot but be considered an area with inherent flaws and questions. Disputes, vagueness, cryptic language, visible and invisible intentions, propaganda, militant speech, all these constitute a field that is appealing but difficult to interpret, as was suggested elsewhere in this book. Having realized the need for an inventive reinforcement of the educational aspect of communication, especially on the level of media discourse, I will offer a few proposals here.

First of all, the nature of media discourse itself as a communication practice is connected, even on a psychoanalytic level, to the recipients and their limits. The audience becomes the analyst on the condition that the outcome for the patients rests on the limits of each analyst. The degrees of perception for each type of content vary depending on the skills, the availability, the ideological load, or the filters that each recipient/unit has among an otherwise manifold audience. This critical parameter targets media discourse as well, which points to the fact that its utterance and transmission is a practice that cannot end on the level of the transmitter. In the case of mass media, despite the fact that journalists or the media appear to be dominant in the communication game, the communication relation that is developed cannot be shrunk within the limits of the message's transmission from the transmitter to the receiver, or by causing a controlled reaction. Without the recipients, without their reaction and reflexes, it will be left hanging, incomplete, unable to leave its mark.

Just as the fate of a message transmitted by the teacher is not only dependent on the knowledge of the transmitter but also on the way a student and potential analyst accepts it, so is the fate of a message transmitted by a journalist dependent on the degree of skill that each of the readers/viewers/listeners has in order to comprehend the message and decode it. Even a copious effort on behalf of the agents of media to orientate the recipients' reactions and then, if possible, to capitalize on and massify their reflexes has to come up against the concept of critical viewing, as long as it has been conquered and depending on the degrees of familiarity and implementation by the recipients. How do the latter react? Passively, critically, just actively, or even effectively?

It is doubtful how serious and efficient it is to choose, with a clear conscience, the role of the expert and to guard that institutional validity. Such a choice presupposes security and magnanimity on behalf of the transmitters, who are called to break free of conventions and potential institutional requirements, thus moving the center of attention from themselves to the others. They have to take up the risk of abandoning their role of "expert" or "superior," of being the ones authorized by a symbolic order and have to challenge the imposition of their "superiority" on those who listen. This is a very risky decision to make, one that leads to an interesting adventure both in the imaginary and in the worldly relation of the speakers to the others.

In this way, is the role of the journalistic subject nullified regarding its relation to the recipients of media discourse? Should the journalists possess what Michel Foucault (1986) calls "the passion of ignorance"? Should they be wishing "no power, a drop of knowledge, a drop of prudence and as much good taste as possible" (Barthes 1964:46)[2]? Should they be worried about their speech, should they be seeking ignorance through active oblivion, should they be shaping the conditions for deliberate and elaborate ignorance?

In my opinion, journalists should welcome ignorance with confidence and a sense of safeness as well as the "unthought of," that which Foucault (1986: 508) defines as the "thought that has not yet seen the light of day." Journalists should abandon the role of the selfish omniscient; they should not be restricted to leading the discursive events but, on the contrary, they should succumb to their flow, they should realize the true meaning of the educational role of their discourse and that, because of this very role, their discourse is simultaneously comprehensible and incomprehensible, truthful and deceptive, promising and self-breaching. I do not support the conscious self-elimination of the subject of speech, considering such a view as eccentric, although it might be fruitful in the field of psychoanalysis. Lastly, in the modern era, challenges are greater and more plentiful. Denying the blind service of profit-driven intentions, resisting the diffusion of oppression, objecting to the facilitation of coercive stances, and a consistent use of language, far from the intentional cultivation of confusion and arbitrary meanings, all these are a few of the more enchanting challenges that have to be faced on a daily basis.

4.2 Dismantling Media "Products" Starting from Childhood

Every individual is the target of various ideological and advertising messages transmitted by modern television from the minute they enter childhood, or even earlier. Protection from the types of discourse and images that serve certain interests should be focused on the development of continuously improving literacy applications for school. The submission and application of proposals regarding the familiarization of children with reading and viewing the media critically can prepare students from an early age for the long road towards the exposure of how the media functions (Tsitsanoudis-Mallidis 2011).

---

[2]   See also Barthes 1973.

The concern regarding the power of media to impose attitudes and behaviors and the association of buying products with the inventiveness or deceitfulness of advertisers in a pointedly commercialized world point to a need for a continuous quest for and formation of imaginative good practices. These practices, however, require a relatively good knowledge of the medium by the educators themselves and their availability to systematically engage with the students on the topic. Such a discussion is part, ideologically speaking, of the so-called critical pedagogy since important questions are posed directly or indirectly. For instance: who benefits from educational mechanisms that accept the status quo? What is the relation between the existing pedagogical practices and education in general and the process of reproducing the system of the dominant class as it is invariably served by the media?

The creation of a "pedagogy of challenge or even resistance," to quote the title of McLaren's and Farahmandpur's book (2013), which refers to models, examples, and interpretations for educators and students that attempt to resist a pointed attack by business interests and their influence on education, remains a continuous desideratum.

Academic preoccupation with issues regarding the sociolinguistic study of media in relation to the reality of school, the development of social and lingual identities of the students and, of course, the positive reinforcement of the students' course towards their further development as active performers of communication (Konstantinidou 2006) has been a major concern for me these past few years. And this is, of course, connected to the dynamic ways of teaching in the classroom and dependent on the reinforcement of cooperative and additive relations (Cummins 2002). Additionally, what should also be utilized—and definitely certainly not ignored—is the previous and usually "heavy" television experience that children bring home from school (Tsitsanoudis-Mallidis 2014).

An effective practice to encourage the receiver as a potential co-creator of communication, in the context of feedback, is to reinforce the promotion of the roles taken up by the students in the context of a school or extracurricular activity, to encourage students to start a communication initiative (Peponis 1974), and to make them engage more often with original linguistic material (Mitsis 2004:198, 230) that can be brought to school by the children.

Besides, the post-print and digital era and the evolving needs created by it can destabilize the traditional views of teaching methods inside the classroom. What is required today of the modern educator is, among other things, the constant and systematic revision of old and stabilized positions and views on reading and writing, with a focus on a more communicative teaching method, even in the field of grammar (Mitsi 2019). Given the fact that the current digital era alters the speed, the value, and the range of information and communication in relation to education, there appears the problem of effectively teaching language lessons that can be done using a series of new post-print literacies. It should be noted that many types of these literacies can be under the umbrella of, or at least connected to, *information literacy*.[3]

The modernization of school regarding the new and sometimes radical methods of knowledge dissemination that are widely used today is of the essence, to the extent that the once dominant teacher-centric and writing-centric methods are considered obsolete and distant from the present requirements. Teaching and familiarizing students with some of the most characteristic kinds of post-print literacies can start at a very early age, as it has been suggested that the efficiency of various programs grows when their implementation starts early on. In other words, children in kindergarten or the first few grades of elementary school are able, as long as they are educated about it, to deal with a medium and its messages in the way they process a new toy: first they look at it with full attention, then they touch and feel it, then they dismantle it, possibly understanding its function and, finally, they try to reassemble it. Extending this analogy to the field of media, I could talk about the process of initially watching a program, decoding its messages, and critically reading them (Konstantinidou 2006).

On the other hand, I can recognize that the concept of literacy is not the same for everyone. Generally speaking, however, it is defined as a grid of explicit and implicit ideological positions on which educational policies are designed and school programs are organized. And, finally, it is through these that the teachers' discourse is created. Also, according to developments in the field of literacy research these past few years, literacy should be examined within a social and cultural context as a practice that has been put in place and not as a neutral skills package that is disconnected from its context (Baynham 2002).

4.3 Readers' Reflexes

Modern readers are called to realize the power of their cultural and social substance since the product of media discourse exercises its commercial appeal and performs its functions not only on the level of ideology but also on the level of consumption with a particular price. In this way, their existence disconnects from the elite capitalists, producers, and distributors and connects to the governed. If receiving media discourse on the part of the recipients/the masses/

---

[3] Over the past few years, there has been an intense utilization and analysis of the so-called electronic text corpora as records of original material. These text corpora have been utilized by linguists to describe and analyze grammars, to study how languages are learned, to form theories on language description, and to write dictionaries and grammars (Michalis 2013:240–262).

the people does not become aligned to their interests, if viewers do not project on it their own expectations and hopes, then media discourse is bound to fail, as Fiske argued in his dissection of the anatomy of television discourse.

From the static conception of a passive recipient, with a series of practices that should not be left to be promoted exclusively by directorial media executives, we could potentially at some point proceed to a conception of the recipient as an active co-creator of communication in the framework of feedback. I would suggest that these practices can be the design of a new media discourse based on each audience, with more live connections to places where groups of citizens gather voluntarily without being told by journalists to do so. It would reinforce the role of witnesses who will not only talk about extreme events, such as a murder or a car accident, but will raise topics that are of a wide social interest. Besides, the ensuing function of feedback is still something that is missing in the modern era in which the imperialistic media have become behemoths.

As for the viewers'/listeners'/readers' attitude against the use of a more vernacularized language, I would like to point out the following: TV viewers ought to stay suspicious and critically deal with the content of the media even when the media discourse they face is based on the vernacular or a vernacularized language. They cannot be left satisfied or flattered because they find that the agents of formal and public discourse talk like them or like the people next door. The presumption of truth, of objectivity, and of social awareness should not be offered easily just because the form and not necessarily the essence of language is vernacular or possesses elements of the so-called low variety against the habits of the social and economic elites. They should not uncritically perceive the use of elements from various geographic or social variations of the formal national language as sufficient proof or redistribution of power among the weak or as if the dominant class has given up its privileges. Democratic legitimacy and social awareness as goods cannot be acquired solely through the form of language but also through the essence of what has been said, with certain practices and measures. They are not presented through the signifiers; they are proven as signified when applied.

In other words, the recipients are obliged not to lose the privilege of objectivity and awareness due to the form of discourse but to find out, on the level of substance, if the claims made through discourse are true.

I believe, however, that it constitutes a kind of success, a kind of victory on the part of the recipients of the lower and middle social strata, that in the official, public discourse of the agents of power there indeed are differentiated voices and an attempt by some to comply with their own unofficial, dialectal linguistic repertoire—even if such a multitude of forms derives from the race for profit and raising advertising revenues or securing funding for a television product. Whatever the criteria or the causes might be, overt or covert, in practice agents of elite media discourse appear willing to enter a process of negotiation of the social identities of their recipients without cancelling or stigmatizing them a priori. In any case, differentiated cultural forms are not underestimated, even the oral ones that are not even documented. So it is proven that the very resistance, conscious or unconscious, on the level of supporting the differentiated cultural forms on the part of recipients, constitutes an alternative form of power, exercised not in a top-down but in a bottom-up direction. The critical treatment of power can thus liberate those who are its subjects and suffer from its discipline.

To conclude, the reaction of readers cannot but connect to the general stance that one ought to have in the face of anything that is expressed by the various establishments and organized systems of privilege. In every form of communication, even in the ostensible communication imposed by the media, those who embody the role of recipient/consumer should pursue what Cummins (2000: 261) calls *authentic critical literacy*, which means to be capable of reading behind the lines, to handle with skepticism the ostensibly benevolent and logical superficial structures, to analyze and process in critical spirit the various statements, and to look for whose interests benefit each time by various forms of communication. The conditions for the restriction and control of *misinformation* and *indoctrination,* which are two of the basic tools for manufacturing consent and ultimately subordination of recipients to the elite narratives, can be developed only in this way.

Since one of the functions of media discourse is the authoritative function that renders the receiver silent due to the nature of this artificial channel that does not favor direct and bidirectional communication, the importance of the reaction of the viewer/recipient is significant. The road of the recipients' passive acceptance and their "submission" to the authorized agent of journalistic authority is the easy way out. The appropriation of a mentality/attitude according to which the so-called consumers of media discourse are controlled by the agents of transmission does not solely disclose a passive self-pity but also a concealed willingness to give up their role as recipients or even to punish themselves for their weakness by bearing the weight of the destroyed polarity of discourse.

Each recipient, each member of the so-called public opinion ought to realize that his/her role against the pluralism of the news is to function as a confrontational force whose culture and social identity are under constant negotiation. This is a negotiation within the reality of television which presupposes the recipients' own participation since it is not a process carried out in their absence but a process ultimately done on their behalf.

In the next sections, I will talk about my own initiatives to contribute to what I see as a connection between education and mass media and their pedagogical and educational function.[4]

4.4 International Summer University: "Greek Language, Culture, and Mass Media"[5]

The idea behind the organization of an International Summer University[6] existed for a long time, and it was sparked by the realization of the power held by the channel of the media and the possibilities of reinforcing its neglected educational function (Chatzisavvidis 2000). Instead of using easy aphorisms about their strengthened ideological and propagandistic function and about the phenomenon of intensive commercialization that occurs in many media (Tsitsanoudis-Mallidis 2011), we chose the hard road of trying to utilize them for educational and pedagogical reasons. At the same time, we also considered the need to serve the purposes of lifelong education and constant educational training as well as the needs of undergraduate and postgraduate students and researchers.

Such was the context in which I designed a program with the general title "Greek Language, Culture and Mass Media" that would expand in time to more specialized topics connected to forms of language in various sociopolitical and cultural conditions, from ancient Greek literature all the way to the present day. The public discussion on a systematic building of bridges and channels of interaction between Greek culture and the modern media, with a focus on the cultivation and dissemination of the Greek language, found willing recipients who were eager to participate. The topics that emerged and were analyzed were original and modern; they included, for example, censorship and the limits of acceptable speech, the connection between ancient Greek literature and journalism, the concept of power and manipulation in classical texts, the errors in language and communication as well as the language of the "other" and the ethics of otherness, thus opening the road for further research and study. This discussion started in a university at the borders of the country, the University of Ioannina, which was called to carry its ideas from Epirus to the Greek islands, thus proving once more that it can escape the narrow limits of its region and country (Tsitsanoudis-Mallidis 2016).

---

[4] See 4.4 and 4.5.
[5] Tsitsanoudis-Mallidis 2019a.
[6] For additional information, please see the Bibliography, Section C, Chapter 4.

4.4.1 International collaborations and special topics

In the five years of the program's existence, we made sure that being open to other organizations was our main priority, creating a tradition of collaborations with prominent international educational, cultural, and media institutions. Thus, the International Summer University (ISU) on Greek Language, Culture, and Mass Media was supported by the Center for Hellenic Studies of Harvard University, the Greek Delegation in the European Parliament, the Association of European Journalists (Greek department), the Orthodox Academy of Crete, the French Department of the European Press Club (Club de la Presse Européenne, Paris), the Centre Culturel Hellénique in Paris as well as the Instituto De Letras of Rio De Janeiro University, the Euro-American Women's Council, the French Embassy in Athens, the Acropolis Museum, the Local Administration etc. The program is under the aegis of the ex-President of the Hellenic Republic (2015-2020), Mr. Prokopis Pavlopoulos, who has been honoring the program with his presence and with his personal lecture to our students for two consecutive years.

The reasons these international collaborations are necessary are connected to our imposed need to develop and cultivate the (inter)national profile of the ISU, its connection with society and the members of the community but also the realization of how useful it is to cooperate with educational and media organizations in order to enrich and examine the initial ideas and concepts more closely. We found that all the organizations and centers that were invited by the Organizing Committee of the ISU to collaborate with it responded with enthusiasm and speed. At the same time, there are even more collaborations in the works with international academic institutions such as the Hellenic Canadian Academic Association of Ontario and others.

Of all the topics the Greek Language, Culture, and Mass Media ISU has touched upon, I will focus on the following:

   a. the language of power during the memorandum days (Second ISU);

   b. censorship against speech and critical thinking; the limits of acceptable speech (Third ISU);

   c. errors in language and communication; contributions and dynamics of deviation (Fourth ISU); and

   d. the language of the "other"; the ethics of otherness (Fifth ISU).[7]

---

[7] I must point out here that the First International Summer University is not mentioned because of its general content which had no clear goals regarding particular topics. Its role, after all, was to chart the academic fields and to function more as a pilot program so that we could surmise

A. The language of power and the memoranda. Regarding the language of power in the days of the memorandum, we focused on the concepts of power and authority as well as the manufacture of consent but also the semantic metaphors in the European press during the era of austerity. We emphasized the reactions of the popular street movements and their linguistic content but also adopted a wider philosophical approach on power and authority in the twenty-first century under the prism of Max Weber. The members of the journalistic community that participated dealt with issues regarding addiction to violence not only in relation to the traditional media but also to social media.

B. Censorship and its limits. Regarding the topic of censorship against speech and critical thinking and the limits of acceptable speech, we addressed specialized topics of great interest. We covered the topics of censorship in public discourse through both a historical and a modern lens, the connection between political censorship and communication, the coercion mechanisms used in censorship by authority as well as the censorship of language in relation to language policy and planning. Furthermore, we examined censorship in music, theater, cartoons, and erotic literature. In the "epilogue" of the program, we talked about critical literacy and critical discourse analysis, specifically targeting the cultivation of critical thought from an ambitious starting point—childhood.

C. Error and its contribution to the evolution of language. From a linguistic perspective, the Fourth ISU was rather focused on issues that were deemed appropriate to the practice of systematic analysis and attentively based on the principles of modern linguistics. It covered topics such as lingual and spelling errors and showed how the science of linguistics deals with error. It also explored spelling as an agent of language memory and examined the most frequent grammatical errors in both oral and written speech by native standard Greek speakers. It posed the question of whether the errors of today tend to become the "rules" of tomorrow, and it also examined closely the most common mistakes in political communication and their influence on manifold audiences. It scrutinized media discourse and the known language/spelling errors that can be found in it, and there were also lectures regarding the influence of mass media on the language of the recipients and the educational function of media discourse. Finally, views were presented on the concept of error in social media and the dynamics and contributions of error in the evolution of language.

---

how much interest there would be in this particular academic initiative, which attempted to connect the media with education, culture, and the Greek language in a more systematic way. What followed came as a real surprise not only to participants but also to the organizers themselves as there was major interest from students both within and outside Greece, a fact that led us to continue and enhance this action.

D. The language of the "other." The questions on language and communication reached their peak at the fifth and most recent ISU. The concept of language of the "other"—the other subject of speech, the different recipient—points to a particularly difficult and obscure field that is equally difficult to approach. If we also consider that the "other" can be anyone that differs from the existing norms, standards, or statuses, anyone that is hidden or is excluded from a given distribution of power to render them unable to bring changes even to their own microcosm, then the size of the challenge can be even larger but also more appealing. It was thus shown that when someone attempts to approach the language of the "other," they may have to accept that they will not be able to completely chart the field if they start from a position that is already finalized, solidified, and permanent. On the contrary, there must be an honest willingness to negotiate and integrate new viewpoints, even uncertainties, in an era that is characterized by fluidity and constant sociopolitical changes.

Keeping this in mind, the Fifth ISU on Greek Language, Culture, and Mass Media attempted to approach the language of the "other" and the ethics of otherness, while acknowledging the fact that it is concurrently a wide and a narrow topic, always relevant and changing with the times. The first thing we addressed was otherness in language, focusing on the island of Lesbos due to the refugee crisis, while also holding a public academic discussion on semantic metaphors and dichotomous discourse about refugees in modern mass media. The dichotomous and racist discourse in the media, with an analysis of hate speech, the positive and negative propaganda, the construction as well as the divisive speech in politics were placed at the very top of the pyramid of the program's scientific interests.[8] The representations of child refugees in journalistic texts as well as the presentation of the parameters that create otherness in Greek language classes in school were also a matter of concern. However, addressing otherness is both about the social assessment and stigmatization of those who are "different," as well as the training of the community on topics regarding how language is connected to concepts such as prestige, glamour, power, and/or authority.

In this context, we discussed topics on "offensiveness" and "destigmatization" in marginal vocabulary, the construction of the "other" through language, the stigmatization of sexual discourse, the "conspiracies" of closed groups as well as identity politics and the problems that accompany it. We also contemplated the issue of "others" in modern Greek theater, where many stories of

---

[8] The students received the *Δημοσιογραφική Κάλυψη Θεμάτων Μετανάστευσης και Μειονοτήτων. Προσέγγιση και Κατευθυντήριες Γραμμές* [Media Coverage of Immigration and Minority Topics: Approach and Guidelines] handbook (2018), a publication of the Respect Words program, followed by a thorough discussion on the Code of Conduct on Fighting the Rhetoric of Hate.

transfers, removals, and meetings are heard. Besides, the language of the theater can be read as a strategic tool of "de-othering" financial and social inequalities.

We also discussed dialects, geographic varieties, and differences on what myths are and are not as well as the use and the role of standard Greek variations, and the lingual and social otherness in Greek names.

In addition, we explored the "other" in new technologies, discussing topics of education on artificial language, communication, and intelligence. There was also a seminar on the language of youth, bloggers, instagrammers, influencers, and social media followers that called upon the audience to take part in this emerging virtual world.

The epilogue of such an action could only pose questions such as: can the language of the other also be my language? How alien can I feel in my own language? How difficult is it to communicate the language of the other, given that every one of us is lonely and seen as the "other" in the eyes of others?[9]

4.4.2 Cultural program and the aesthetic view

Besides the strict academic daily schedule (whose total duration was forty hours), all five International Summer University seminars were accompanied by an equally diverse cultural schedule. Beyond the academic setting and the perfect organization characterized as such by the press which allowed no deviations from a program planned with tenacity and attention to detail months before, the students were urged to get to know the cultural identity of the space they were in. In the context of an unending desire for improvement, we believed that a summer university can be more prone and open to interdisciplinary approaches, in comparison to what can occur in an auditorium where specialization is usually dominant. At the same time, and after careful planning, this summer academic activity became a permanent workshop that offered the students and researchers the possibility to experience unknown aspects of the topics that emerge through scientific discourse.[10]

---

[9] See also Tsitsanoudis-Mallidis 2019a and 2019b.

[10] For example, in the summer of 2017, there was a seminar on censorship in daily cartoons and, at the same time, a gallery exhibited drawings by the most important Greek cartoonists. The aim here was to help students interact with the creators of the drawings. Such encounters had already begun in previous years like when eminent Greek film directors such as Pantelis Voulgaris in Andros and Giannis Smaragdis in Crete visited the seminars. Vassilis Lekkas also gave a concert outside a chapel on the island held for the entertainment of the participants, which proved to be a wonderful listening experience for the young people who attended. Amazing cultural happenings were also held in Syros, which has a rich cultural tradition, and kept the participants entertained (ancient tragedies performances, *rembetika* concerts, organ concerts in the cathedral etc.).

In other words, we focused on getting the students acquainted with the history of the island, its identity, and its distinguished creators. The fact that the students were able to participate in the educational process through workshops and essay presentations in an environment of cooperation and mutual reinforcement was also very important. Current affairs were put under scrutiny, and we sought feedback from academic discourse with texts and experiences written by the hundreds of students. For example, I will mention the emotional report prepared by students of the Second International Summer University on the issue of immigration and the experiences shared by the people who worked or volunteered at the hot spots. I should also point out that all the presentations from the brainstorming session of the Fifth ISU are published in the Ελληνικό Βλέμμα (Greek Gaze) journal by the Instituto De Letras of the Federal University of Rio De Janeiro.

Finally, emphasis was placed on the aesthetics of the brochure and the materials of the program.[11] A collective volume came out recently by Gutenberg Publications titled Ελληνική Γλώσσα, Πολιτισμός και ΜΜΕ [Greek Language, Culture and Mass Media] (Tsitsanoudis-Mallidis 2017c) that includes the lectures of the first two International Summer Universities as well as studies and articles by eminent professors from universities in Greece, Harvard, and Rio de Janeiro. Another collective volume is currently in the works titled Το Λάθος στη Γλώσσα και την Επικοινωνία [Error in Language and Communication] (forthcoming).

4.4.3 Conclusions

Hundreds of people including eminent academics from Greece and foreign universities, scholars, journalists, artists, authors, and researchers as well as prominent businessmen as sponsors shared our goals and actively participated in the evolution and enrichment of our original vision to systematically connect the media to the Greek language and culture. Academic knowledge was only strengthened by an aesthetic perception that would improve the content through an elegant form.

Not only did the media, both Greek and international, not ignore this initiative as a cynic would predict but, on the contrary, they were happy to offer their help and support. They showed fast reflexes by promoting, along with many universities in the country, all five events. In the past three years, the ISU had the Hellenic Broadcasting Corporation (ERT) as its sponsor of communication and, in particular, ERT3 and the First Station of Greek Radio as well as the

---

[11] The printed materials of the program were designed at Gutenberg Publications by Mr. Giannis Mamais, to whom we are deeply grateful.

Parliament's TV channel. TV advertisements were shot to promote the event with prominent Greek actors and journalists as protagonists.

Behind all these collaborations stand all the people who believed in this initiative and worked to keep everyone's spirits high. This is a program whose creative team, under the supervision of an international scientific committee, works for a year in order to organize just a week full of summer classes that support the Greek language and culture in modern Greek and European media, and its goal is to keep improving. Besides, the very recent founding of the ISU Greek Language, Culture, and Mass Media Alumni Club seems to validate the program and ask for its continuation with the participation of young people, which is the central axis of every academic action. Knowing how big a responsibility it is to organize the ISU, every year the ISU organizers try their best to open up new research avenues and to offer the Greek and foreign participants a useful and exciting experience worthy of an academic experience of the highest standards (Tsitsanoudis-Mallidis 2016).

4.5 Language and Communication Mini Seminars of the Hellenic Broadcasting Corporation

The discourse transmitted by electronic media, and especially the radio, is characterized by simplification and quite often becomes a typical example of the use of slogans. It is also full of errors that, when transmitted through a powerful channel, can influence audiences and regulate subsequent uses and forms of language.

I had the honor of designing and holding the position of scientific consultant of the Language and Communication Mini Seminars,[12] which were organized by the Hellenic Broadcasting Corporation (ERT) and the schools of Educational Sciences and the Pedagogy Department for Kindergarten Teachers at the University of Ioannina with the collaboration and participation of professors in Greek and foreign universities. The aim was to train journalists, presenters, editors, and generally designers of media discourse in issues that have to do with the uses of the Greek language through workshops and classes with constant interaction with the teacher and discussions about the "errors" in the use of language on the level of the public sphere of media discourse.

---

[12] The mini seminars were first held for two years at the Pedagogy Department for Kindergarten Teachers at the University of Ioannina and addressed the students at the university. During the academic year 2019–2020, the same activity was organized by the same department in collaboration with the Journalists Union of the Peloponnese, Epirus, and the Islands.

The mini seminars addressed the errors in language by the agents of media discourse.[13] Two weekly cycles of classes on grammar, spelling, and syntax were organized for the employees at ERT in order to enrich their knowledge in these particular fields. The mini seminars took place during the academic year 2016–2017. The first cycle was for the ERT employees in Athens and the second for the ERT employees in northern Greece. Attending the seminars was compulsory. The lecturers were university teachers and lecturers from Greek and foreign universities. The project was directed academically by a scientific committee whose members were all university professors. The topics included in the seminars were the following:

- Informed or uninformed? Usual deviations from correct verbal types (regarding production and etymology)
- Language errors in print and electronic media and their influence on readers and viewers
- Online use of language, especially in social media
- Spelling points; capital letters and their correct use
- *Greeklish*: the Greek case of Homo Flexibilis
- Conjugation and production of modern Greek language
- Language questions: choosing the proper verbal form
- Problematic cases of combining verbs
- Errors of today, rules of tomorrow?

These seminars showed that spelling skills are indicative of linguistic quality since they are an important component of a person's language competence. However, spelling cannot be conquered with communicative processes but with traditional teaching and exercise that can lead the speakers from the realization of the principles of the spelling system to a stage of automatic implementation. The highly conventional character of spelling and the Greek language's special history do not favor the creation and acceptance of a unified and generally

---

[13] These are errors in spelling, reading, listening, and utterance but also errors in comprehension and communication. The errors of the language area include the phonological, morphological, syntactical and semantic errors, mixes and corruptions, errors in word choice and written errors. The fields of sociolinguistics and dialectology include the individual and group deviations from the standard Greek language. Errors in communications are the violations of truth axioms and informativity. There are also errors on the language level and on the level of linguistic analysis. In addition, there are the justified mistakes that happen and which go unnoticed as well as errors that never happen. Finally, there is another category of interesting errors that belong in psycholinguistics (for example, errors due to emotional tension) (Setatos, 1991).

accepted spelling system. However, these different perceptions and views on language are quite often rather beneficial because they maintain our interest for the language and contribute to a deeper study and more effective learning. To sum up, the issue of spelling is a complicated issue because, apart from the purely linguistic aspects and the difficulties it presents, it is also connected to additional ideological, political, emotional, social, aesthetic, and other factors.

Just like in grammar, some of the errors in spelling lead to a simplification of the system and are sometimes adopted by more and more users, thus leading to changes that will be generalized through time and imposed as normal in the standard form of the written language (Mitsis 2017).

4.6 Asserting the Aesthetic Function

The educational role of media which, even if it is considered nowadays as a secondary function, should be connected more tightly and systematically to the aesthetic function. The search for Nietzsche's morality of the future in the public sphere, and especially in highly ideologically charged discourses such as political and media discourse, remains a desideratum. "No practical action is destined to lack aesthetic function, which is inherent, at least potentially, in every human action," writes Mukarovsky.[14] And he goes on to explain that in the case of language, every process that showcases its semantic relations, which organize the context, can cause an aesthetic function. He also mentions that a strong simile, an antithesis, an impressive phonetic similarity as well as an unexpected flip in the sequence of words can cause a shudder of aesthetic pleasure.

It is not my intention, nor do I possess the necessary knowledge, to delve into this subject, but I do believe that a brief mention would be very useful here. The reason I take the risk of raising this topic just before the end of the book is precisely because I wish to put the entirety of this essay under the prism of aesthetics, as if I am trying to undermine every opinion that has been expressed thus far.

Whether we're talking about the beautiful or the unsightly, the search for criteria has always been a goal for artists, philosophers, and scholars who have tried in vain to set down criteria, rules, standards and common perceptions. The standards for what is beautiful and what is not seem to be changing with time and among cultures and an "ecumenical" perception seems to be impossible (Christakos 2019). Recognizing what we characterize as beautiful, both in nature and art, urges us to seek the approval or disapproval of the other,

---

[14] See Murakovsky 1979 for a link to an electronic version of the article.

the opposite, the non-beautiful. The beautiful or the unsightly are inextricably linked to the aesthetic phenomenon and its function both from the perspective of the artist–creator and from the perspective of the viewer–recipient. But how can this aesthetic phenomenon be influenced? It is generally accepted that factors such as race and culture, the natural environment and climate, historical circumstances, the level of knowledge, experience, and available information, social and economic class can shape the aesthetic criteria of both subjects—the creator and the viewer (Christakos 2019).

While searching online for descriptions and depictions of the relation between the aesthetic function and mass media, I found very few results since the pieces of knowledge that link the media with aesthetics are limited but valuable nevertheless.[15] As a result, I will not in any way attempt to assess the implementation of the aesthetic function or lack thereof; conversely, I will choose to propagate what is positive and what should be sought after. I believe that it is imperative that we show a certain type of stubbornness in implementing the aesthetic function and perspective in media texts of all kinds in order to deal with some of the most repulsive aspects of electronic digitization and word processing software. And while the demand for the cultivation of visual and informational literacy has risen these past few years, the mentions of the value of good taste and aesthetic perfection are fewer, something that should have benefitted from—not been diminished by—the speed and ease that technology provides us. The concept of harmony as a dominant parameter in the laborious process of negotiation between the creator and the reader needs to be promoted and elevated to the public sphere. Industrialized production might often lack in aesthetic value, taking away from beauty the purity and potential that it deserves. Consequently, a series of aesthetic errors are perpetuated and cultivated, which possibly "educate" the manifold readership to develop questionable taste at the expense of aesthetic quality.

The daily fight for the concept of beauty against the tyranny of speed or the dominance of profit has been a necessity from the times of medieval miniaturists to the digital flat screen of an iPhone. The constant resistance against anything that "bitters the sight" requires a reflection on terms such as pulchritude, aesthetic pleasure, artistic beauty, classic form, smooth, and beautiful texts (Mamais 2019).

"Form is solidified deeply in the aesthetic perception of the reading public, to a degree that when the readers are asked to assess a tasteful text, they miss it or pass it indifferently. And while the ease of electronic realities has put an

---

[15] There are some media and communications departments in Greece where there are modules called Aesthetics and Communication and Aesthetics of Advertising.

end to the difficulties of the past, the misfortune of sloppiness is still going strong in many cases. The automated functions of machines have replaced the refined taste and the resourcefulness of experienced designers." (Mamais 2019). And if it is imperative for modern readers to reflect on the image of books, it is even more useful to seek the high forms and aesthetic perceptions in media discourse, both on a semantic and on a formal level.

Epilogue

MEDIA DISCOURSE nowadays seems to, on the one hand, promise subversion of the status quo and the powers that derive from it and, on the other hand, to break that promise since it preserves or appears to preserve all the proper ties that derive from being a part of the establishment.

According to Fairclough, there are no innocent texts, and no text is free of the pressures of the sociocultural context.

The media discourse fragments that were studied for the purpose of this book from 1974 and onwards verified this view, unveiling the fact that language as a living organism depicted and consistently followed the crucial political, economic, and generally cultural transformations that defined the course of Greek society. Language became more popular—it was vernacularized—because that was the political atmosphere created by the restoration of democracy. It assumed progressive connotations through its distancing from the formal style because this process facilitated the concentration around certain political parties and aroused popular expectations. It acquired even more popular characteristics when private media sought to open up to wider populations within Greek society. It affected and was affected by the tight embrace of the political and television/publishing establishment. It lost and regained the emblematic role of representing the popular movements. Finally, in the era of MoUs (2009–2018), it became a sharp tool used to incriminate and manipulate in order to serve the goal of supporting the government through evoking fear and the manufacturing of consent for the tyrannical measures imposed on the Greek people.

By means of metaphoric discourse, citizens were called to accept and compromise as an "inferiority" against the political and economic intrusion of "superior" capitalists. The clear meanings of words were lost in an atmosphere of oppression, which was unanimously engineered by part of the media, while the frenetic rhythm of the digital age established new meanings and contents which were cemented in a fast-track fashion due to social media.

As a person that served in the media for over twenty years and was privileged enough to enter the academic community thereafter, I still feel puzzled, leaving the questions I included in the epilogue of my doctoral dissertation unanswered (Tsitsanoudis-Mallidis 2005).[1]

Who is the central agent of power who regulates—philosophically, politically, socially—the extent of media's superpower? How democratic are the forces of control and formation of the form and content of a biased discourse like media discourse? Is it indeed coercive, a discourse which is reduced to a product of commercial transaction like so many other contemporary commercial cultural commodities? Is it possible that we should not just talk of fictive sympathy but also of excessive compliance of the "elite" journalist with the "common" viewers in favor of advertising and profit? Finally, how educational can the character of a discourse be when it is undermined by the domination of the propagandist function, eliminating the democratic nature of the social good?

Is it possible that transmitters and recipients dominate one another in the contemporary information society, delimiting the hopes for a true and meaningful relationship of feedback, a relationship which could liberate forces and collectivities in order to cooperate with each other to create more caring societies which, among other things, would respect the environment more as well?

These are questions I agonized over throughout the whole of this research, while observing the two poles of communication: a) the recipients, who realize the existence of a series of restrictions that restrain the development of a true relationship of feedback with news media, which constantly augment their power and b) the producers of media discourse, who react because they are often obliged to align their discourse and topics with the needs of each sample of viewership measurements (which often hang as the sword of Damocles over the existence of their very public presence) or to the directions of their proprietors and of financial credit power centers.

Within such a framework, I believe that it is not legitimate to speak of meaningful *collaborative* relations between the media or journalists and the recipients of their discourse nor of a meaningful process of feedback between them. Subsequently, I conclude with the observation that we face a distortion of the news/information system due to the prioritization of economic interests of which, surprisingly, both poles of communication suffer the consequences.

I insist, though, that any proposal could not possibly be restricted to the cultivation and enrichment of critical thinking on the part of the readers. There is a need for a step beyond that which is, in my view, the development

---

[1] My dissertation is titled *The Use of Modern Greek and Media Discourse: The Nature, Functions, and Educational Importance of Modern Television Discourse.* My supervisor was Professor Napoleon Mitsis to whom I owe my academic identity and gratitude.

of individual confidence and creativity, the faith, in other words, that one can bring about radical changes to the status quo of their time, commencing from its very microcosmos and, of course, meaningful collectivities are required.

It is a constant battle with language itself as a leading tool in the arsenal, which can restructure reality if it is not abandoned in favor of image regardless of how tough or fluid these realities might always be.

Bibliography

A. Greek References

Androutsopoulos, G. 2001. "Γλωσσολογικές προσεγγίσεις στον δημοσιογραφικό λόγο. Είδη, ποικιλότητα και ιδεολογία" [Linguistic approaches to media discourse: Types, variety and ideology]. In Boukalas and Moschonas 2001:67–183.

Babiniotis, G. 1994. *Ελληνική γλώσσα: Παρελθόν-παρόν-μέλλον* [Greek language: Past-present-future]. Athens.

Barthes, R. 1973. *Μυθολογίες, μάθημα* [Mythologies, lesson]. Athens.

Baynham, M. 2002. *Πρακτικές γραμματισμού* [Literacy practices]. Trans. M. Arapopoulou. Athens.

Boukalas, P. and S. Moschonas, eds. 2001. *Δημοσιογραφία και γλώσσα* [Journalism and language]. Athens.

Chatzisavvidis, S. 2000. *Ελληνική γλώσσα και δημοσιογραφικός λόγος. Θεωρητικές και ερμηνευτικές προσεγγίσεις* [Greek language and journalistic discourse: Theoretical and research approaches]. Athens.

Chomsky, N. 1987. *Η χειραγώγηση των μαζών - Συνεντεύξεις με τον David Barsamian.* [Manipulating the masses: Interviews with David Barsamian]. Athens.

Christakos, G. 2019. *Σκέψεις για το ωραίο και μη-ωραίο. Ανέκδοτο κείμενο.* [Thoughts on the beautiful and non-beautiful]. Unpublished.

Christidis, A., and M. Theodoropoulou, eds. 2001. *Εγκυκλοπαιδικός οδηγός για τη γλώσσα* [Encyclopedic guide on language]. Centre for the Greek Language. pg. 311, 316. Thessaloniki.

Cummins, J. 2002. *Ταυτότητες υπό διαπραγμάτευση* [Negotiating identities]. Trans. S. Argyri. Athens.

Denaxa, M. 2019. "Προπαγάνδα, αυτή η 'άλλη' επικοινωνία" [Propaganda, that "other" communication]. Lecture given at the Fifth International Summer University of the University of Ioannina, Syros, July 8–15.

Diamantakou, P. 2001. "Τα στερεότυπα και η λατρεία του τηλεοπτικού λόγου." [Stereotypes and the worship of television discourse]. In Boukalas and Moschonas 2001.

Dictionary of Standard Modern Greek. [Λεξικό τῆς Κοινῆς Νεοελληνικῆς], 2nd ed. 2001. Thessaloniki.

Dizelos, Th. 1976. *Γλώσσα και δημοσιογραφία* [Language and journalism]. Athens.

Eco, U. n.d. *Η σημειολογία στην καθημερινή ζωή* [Semiology of everyday life]. Trans. A. Tsopanoglou, ed. I. Theodoros. Thessaloniki.

Filippakis, G. 2004. *Ανέκδοτη έκθεση απόψεων για τον τηλεοπτικό δημοσιογραφικό λόγο* [Unpublished manuscript on views on media discourse]. Available from N. Tsitsanoudis-Mallidis.

Fiske, J. 2000. *Η ανατομία του τηλεοπτικού λόγου* [The anatomy of television discourse]. Trans. V. Spyropoulou. Athens. Orig. pub. as *Reading Television*. London/New York, 1978.

Fitoussi, J. P. (2021). *Τι μας κρύβουν οι λέξεις. Πώς η νεογλώσσα επηρεάζει τις κοινωνίες μας.* [What the words hide from us. How neo-language affects our societies]. Trans. A. Papagiannidis. Athens.

Fragkoudaki, A. 1999. *Γλώσσα και Ιδεολογία* [Language and ideology]. Athens.

Foucault, M. 1986. *Οι λέξεις και τα πράγματα* [The order of things]. Trans. K. Papagiorgis. Athens.

Gavriilidou, Z. 2017. *Οι εννοιολογικές μεταφορές στον τύπο την εποχή της λιτότητας* [Semantic metaphors in the press during the age of austerity]. In *Ελληνική γλώσσα, επικοινωνία και ΜΜΕ* [Greek language, communication and mass media], ed. N. Tsitsanoudis-Mallidis, 200–224. Athens.

Georgakopoulou, A. and D. Goutsos. 1999. *Κείμενο και επικοινωνία* [Text and communication]. Athens.

Gotovos, T. 1996. *Ρατσισμός: κοινωνικές, ψυχολογικές και παιδαγωγικές όψεις μιας ιδεολογίας και μιας πρακτικής.* [Racism: social, psychological and educational aspects of an ideology and a practice]. Athens.

Goutsos, D. 2017. *Ο αντίλογος των πλατειών και ο λόγος των ΜΜΕ στην Ελλάδα της κρίσης* [The response of the squares and media discourse in Greece during the crisis]. In *Ελληνική γλώσσα, πολιτισμός και ΜΜΕ. Από την αρχαιοελληνική γραμματεία έως σήμερα.* [Greek language, communication and mass media: From ancient literature until today], ed. N. Tsitsanoudis-Mallidis, 346–387. Athens.

Konstantinidou, Ch. 2006. *Το ζήτημα της αγωγής στα ΜΜΕ σε ιστορική προοπτική. Από τον παθητικό καταναλωτή στον ενεργό επιτελεστή* [The issue of media education in historical perspective: From passive consumer to active participant]. *Ζητήματα επικοινωνίας* [Communication matters] 4:18–40.

Kostoula-Makraki, N. 2001. *Γλώσσα και κοινωνία. Βασικές έννοιες.* [Language and society: Basic concepts]. Athens.

Koutsoulelou-Mihou, S. 1997. *Η γλώσσα της διαφήμισης.* [The language of advertising]. Athens.

Kyrtsos, G. 2003. *Ο μυστικός πόλεμος των εξουσιών.* [The secret war between powers]. Athens.

Lascaratou, Ch. 2012. "Η λειτουργία της γλώσσας στη βιωματική εμπειρία του πόνου σε διαλόγους θεραπευτών–ασθενών" [The function of language in the experience of pain from dialogues between therapists and patients]. In Tsitsanoudis-Mallidis 2012b:17–40.

Mamais, G. 2019. "Από την παραδοσιακή τυπογραφία στις νέες τεχνολογίες. Υπάρχουν σήμερα όμορφα βιβλία;" [From traditional typography to new technologies: Are there any beautiful books today?]. Lecture given at Athens College, Athens, May 10. https://www.blod.gr/lectures/apo-tin-paradosiaki-typografia-stis-nees-tehnologies-yparhoun-simera-omorfa-biblia/.

McLaren, P. and R. Farahmandpur. 2013. *Για μια παιδαγωγική της αντίστασης. Διδάσκοντας ενάντια στον παγκόσμιο καπιταλισμό και τον νέο ιμπεριαλισμό* [Teaching against global capitalism and the new imperialism: A critical pedagogy]. Trans. K. Therianos. Athens.

Michalis, A. 2013. "Αξιοποίηση των ηλεκτρονικών σωμάτων κειμένων στη διδασκαλία της γραμματικής: Μεθοδολογικές αρχές και πρακτική εφαρμογή" [Utilizing electronic text corpora in teaching grammar: Methodological principles and practice]. In *Γλώσσα και σύγχρονη (πρωτο) σχολική εκπαίδευση. Επίκαιρες προκλήσεις και προοπτικές* [Language and modern school education: Current challenges and perspectives], ed. N. Tsitsanoudis-Mallidis, 241–265. Athens.

Mitsi, A. 2019. *Η συμβολή της γραμματικής στην ανάπτυξη της επικοινωνιακής ικανότητας των μαθητών: παρουσίαση πειραματικής εφαρμογής με βάση τις αρχές της επικοινωνιακής- κειμενοκεντρικής προσέγγισης στην Ε' Δημοτικού* [The contribution of grammar to the development of pupils' communication competence: presenting an experimental teaching on the 5th grade of primary education, based on the principles of the communicative text-centered approach]. Doctoral diss., University of Ioannina. https://www.didaktorika.gr/eadd/handle/10442/45863

Mitsis, N. 1999. *Διδακτική του γλωσσικού μαθήματος. Από τη γλωσσική θεωρία στη διδακτική πράξη.* [Teaching language lessons: From language theory to teaching practices]. Athens.

———. 2000. *Στοιχειώδεις αρχές και μέθοδοι της εφαρμοσμένης γλωσσολογίας. Εισαγωγή στη διδασκαλία της Ελληνικής ως δεύτερης (ή ξένης) γλώσσας* [Basic principles and methods of applied linguistics: Introduction to teaching Greek as a second (or foreign) language]. 1st ed. 1998. Athens.

———. 2004. *Η διδασκαλία της γλώσσας υπό το πρίσμα της επικοινωνιακής προσέγγισης* [Teaching language under the prism of the communicational approach]. Athens.

———. 2017. Foreword to *Μικρά σεμινάρια γλώσσας και επικοινωνίας* [Mini Seminars on language and communication,] ed. N. Tsitsanoudis-Mallidis. Athens.

Moschonas, S. 1995. "Ακροατήρια και επικοινωνία" [Audiences and communication]. *Διαβάζω* [Diavazo] 348:182–188. Athens.

———. 2005. *Ιδεολογία και γλώσσα* [Ideology and language]. Athens.

Mukarovsky, J. 1979. "Ο ποιητικός προσδιορισμός και η αισθητική λειτουργία της γλωσσας" [The poetic definition and the aesthetic function of language]. *Deukalion* 8:114-121. https://doi.org/10.26220/deu.1466.

Orwell, G. 1999. *1984. Ο Μεγάλος Αδελφός* [1984: Big Brother]. Trans. N. Barti. Athens.

Papadimitriou, Z. 2012. "Πολιτικό σύστημα, τηλεόραση και διαχείριση του ανθρώπινου πόνου" [Political system, television and human pain management]. In Tsitsanoudis-Mallidis 2012b:107–115.

Papadopoulou-Mantathaki, S. 2019. *Η γλώσσα του πόνου και οι μεταφορές της. Από την παιδική ηλικία στην ενηλικίωση* [The language of pain and its metaphors: From childhood to adulthood]. Athens.

Papanoutsos, E. 2008. "Η φθορά των λέξεων–Το δίκαιο της στιγμής" [The decay of words: The right of the moment] In *Θεματικοί κύκλοι*, 20–21. Athens.

Peponis, A. 1974. *Η μεγάλη επικοινωνία* [The great communication]. Athens.

———. 2006. Introduction to Tsitsanoudis-Mallidis 2006:19–23.

Politis, P. 2001. "Μέσα μαζικής ενημέρωσης: Το επικοινωνιακό πλαίσιο και η γλώσσα τους" [Mass media: The communicational framework and its language]. In Christidis 2001: 114–120.

Respect Words. 2018. *Δημοσιογραφική κάλυψη θεμάτων μετανάστευσης και μειονοτήτων. Προσέγγιση και κατευθυντήριες γραμμές* [Media coverage of immigration and minority topics: Approach and guidelines]. Athens.

Semoglou, O. 2001. "Γλώσσα της εικόνας και εκπαίδευση" [Language of the image and education] In *Εγκυκλοπαιδικός οδηγός για τη γλώσσα* [Encyclopedic guide on language]. In Christidis 2001:270–274.

Setatos, M. 1978. "Το γλωσσικό ζήτημα και η καθιέρωση της δημοτικής στο πλαίσιο της γενικής γλωσσολογίας" [The language question and the institution of the demotic in the context of general linguistics]. In *Για τη Δημοτική γλώσσα* [About the Demotic language], 81-87. Athens.

———. 1991. "Τα γλωσσικά λάθη και η αντιμετώπισή τους» [Language errors and their treatment]. *Φιλόλογος* 63:17-39.

Triantafyllidis, M. 1963. "Ξενηλασία ή ισοτέλεια: Μελέτη περί των ξένων λέξεων της Νέας Ελληνικής" [Pogrom or equality: A study of foreign words in standard Greek] Vol. 1 of *Απαντα* [Complete Works]. Thessaloniki.

Tsitsanoudis-Mallidis, N. 2005. *Η χρήση της Νεοελληνικής Γλώσσας και ο δημοσιογραφικός λόγος - Η φύση, οι λειτουργίες και η παιδευτική σημασία του σύγχρονου τηλεοπτικού δημοσιογραφικού λόγου.*[The use of Modern Greek Language and the journalistic discourse: The nature, the functions and the educative meaning of the current televisional journalistic discourse]. PhD diss., University of Thessaly.

———. 2006. *Η λαϊκή γλώσσα των ειδήσεων-Μια στάση απατηλής οικειότητας.* [The popular language of the news: An attitude of illusive intimacy]. Athens.

———. 2011. *Η γλώσσα της εξουσίας στις ημέρες του μνημονίου* [The language of authority in the days of the memorandum]. Athens.

———. 2012a. "Γλώσσα και διεκπεραίωση των αιτημάτων 'του κόσμου' στον δημόσιο λόγο" [Language and fulfillment of people's demands in public discourse]. In *Η διαχείριση του πόνου στη δημόσια σφαίρα - Από τη νηπιακή ηλικία έως την ενηλικίωση* [Pain management in the public sphere: From infancy to adulthood]. Athens.

———, ed. 2012b. *Η διαχείριση του πόνου στη δημόσια σφαίρα - Από τη νηπιακή ηλικία έως την ενηλικίωση* [Pain management in the public sphere: From infancy to adulthood], 89–105. Athens.

———2013. "Χαρακτηριστικά του δημόσιου λόγου σε απεικονίσεις της οικονομικής κρίσης στην Ελλάδα" [Public discourse characteristics in representations of the financial crisis in Greece]. *Γλωσσολογία* 21:39-55.

———2016. *Γέφυρες και Δίαυλοι. Ελληνική Γλώσσα, Πολιτισμός και Μέσα Μαζικής Επικοινωνίας.* [Bridges and channels. Greek language, culture, and mass media]. Ioannina.

———, ed. 2017a. *Ελληνική Γλώσσα, Πολιτισμός και ΜΜΕ: Από την Αρχαιοελληνική Γραμματεία έως σήμερα* [Greek Language, Culture and Media: From the Ancient Greek Literacy to the present]. Athens.

———. 2017b. "Οι γιατροί και οι ασθενείς των μνημονίων" [The doctors and patients of the memoranda]. In *Ελληνική γλώσσα, πολιτισμός και ΜΜΕ* [Greek language, culture and mass media]. Athens.

————. 2018. "Νεολογισμοί της δημόσιας σφαίρας: Από τη βάσανο της χρήσης στην ταχεία ωρίμανση των 'Trumponomics': Μια προσέγγιση με ιδεολογικό προσανατολισμό" [Neologisms in the public sphere: From the check of the use to the fast maturity of "Trumponomics": An approach with an ideological focus] In *Figura in praesentia*, ed. K. Ntinas, 564-580. Athens.

————. 2019. "Greek Language, Culture and Mass Media: The Philosophy and Direction of an International Summer University." Presented at the First Interdisciplinary Conference on Sports and Art: Scientific and Artistic Dialogue, University of Ioannina, April 5-7.

Tsitsanoudis-Mallidis, N. and E. Theodoropoulos, 2015. "The Use of Dialectal Varieties in Modern Advertising—Ideological Ramification." In *Teaching Modern Greek Language Varieties and Dialects in Primary and Secondary Education. Theoretical Approaches and Teaching Applications*, ed. M. Tzakosta. Athens.

Tsokalidou, R. 2001. "Θέματα κοινωνιογλωσσολογίας για δημοσιογράφους" [Sociolinguistics topics for journalists]. In *Εφαρμοσμένη γλωσσολογία* [Applied linguistics] 17:109–116. Thessaloniki.

Tzannetakos, G. nd. *Λόγος Ελληνικός στη δημοσιογραφία.* [Greek speech in journalism]. Athens.

Valiouli, M. 2001. "Υπερβολές, αυθαιρεσίες και νοηματικές εκπτώσεις" [Exaggerations, indiscretions and semantic compromises]. In *Εφαρμοσμένη γλωσσολογία* [Applied linguistics] 17: 9–26. Thessaloniki.

B. Non-Greek References

Allan, K. and K. Burridge. 2006. *Forbidden Words: Taboo and the Censoring of Language.* New York.

Bakhtin, N. 1981. *The Dialogic Imagination: Four Essays*, ed. M. Holquist, trans. M. Holquist and C. Emerson. Austin.

Barthes, R. 1964. *Le degré zéro de l'écriture* [Writing degree zero]. Orig. pub. in French, 1953. Paris.

Benveniste, E. 1966. *Problèmes de linguistique générale 1.* Paris.

Chomsky, N. 1965. *Aspects of the Theory of Syntax.* Cambridge, MA.

———. 1987. *The Manufacture of Consent.* New York.

Clayman, S. 1991. "News Interview Openings: Aspects of Sequential Organization." In Scannell 1991:48-75.

Corson, D. 1993. *Language, Minority Education and Gender: Linking Social Justice and Power.* Clevedon.

Coupland, N. and H. Giles, eds. 1988. "Communication Accommodation Theory: Recent Developments." *Language and Communication*, vol. 8.

De Beaugrande, R. 2001. "Large Corpora, Small Corpora, and the Learning of 'Language.'" In *Small Corpus Studies and ELT*, ed. M. Ghadessy, A. Henry, and R.L. Roseberry, 3–28. Amsterdam.

De Bleser, R. and C. Kauschke. 2003. "Acquisition and Loss of Nouns and Verbs: Parallel or Divergent Patterns?" *Journal of Neurolinguistics* 16:213–229.

Deignan, A. 2005. *Metaphor and Corpus Linguistics.* Amsterdam.

Ducrot, O. (1980). *Dire et ne pas dire: principes de sémantique linguistique.* Paris.

Fairclough, N. 1989. *Language and Power.* London and New York.

———. 1995. *Media Discourse.* London.

———. 2003. *Analysing Discourse.* London.

Ferguson, C. A. 1964. "Baby Talk in Six Languages" *American Anthropologist* 66:103-114.

Fiske, S. T. and S. E. Taylor. 1991. *Social Cognition: From Brains to Culture.* 2nd ed. New York.

Fowler, R. 1991. *Language in News. Discourse and Ideology in the Press.* London.

Giles, H., R. Y. Bourhis and D. M. Taylor. 1977. "Towards a Theory of Language in Ethnic Group Relations." In *Language, Ethnicity and Intergroup Relation*, ed. H. Giles. London.

Goffman, E. 1981. *Forms of Talk.* Philadelphia.

Greatbatch, D. 1992. "On the Management of Disagreement Between News Interviewees." In *Talk at Work: Interaction in Institutional Settings*, ed. P. Drew and J. Heritage, 268-301. New York.

Grimes, J. 1975. *The Thread of Discourse*. The Hague.

Gwyn, R. 1999. "Captain of My Own Ship: Metaphor and the Discourse of Chronic Illness." In *Researching and Applying Metaphor*, ed. L. Cameron and G. Low, 203-220. Cambridge.

Heritage, J. and D. Greatbatch. 1991. "On the Institutional Character of Institutional Talk." In *Talk and Social Structure: Studies in Ethnography and Conversation Analysis*, ed. D. Boden and D.H. Zimmerman, 93-137. Cambridge.

Jucker, A. 1992. *Social Stylistics: Syntactic Variation in British Newspapers*. Berlin.

Kress, G. 1996. "Representational Resources and the Production of Subjectivity: Questions for the Theoretical Development of Critical Discourse Analysis in a Multicultural Society." In *Texts and Practices: Reading in Critical Discourse Analysis*, ed. C.R. Caldas-Coulthard and M. Coulthard, 15-31. London.

Lascaratou, C. 2008. "The Function of Language in the Experience of Pain." In *Reconstructing Pain and Joy: Linguistic, Literary, and Cultural Perspectives.*, ed. C. Lascaratou, A. Despotopoulou, and E. Ifantidou, 35–37. Newcastle.

Lascaratou, C. and S. Marmaridou. 2005. "Metaphor in Greek Pain Constructions: Cognitive and Functional Perspectives." In *Reviewing Linguistic Thought: Converging Trends for the 21st Century*, ed. S. Marmaridou, K. Nikiforidou, and E. Antonopoulou, 235–254. Berlin.

Levinson, S. C. 1988. "Putting Linguistics on a Proper Footing: Explorations." In *Erving Goffman: Exploring the Interaction Order*, ed. P. Drew and A. Wootton, 165-174. Boston.

Lippmann, W. 1979. *Making the News*. London.

Livingstone, S. and P. Lunt. 1994. *Talk on Television*. London.

Pavlenko, A. 2002. "Emotions and the Body in Russian and English." *Pragmatics and Cognition* 10n1–2:207–241.

Saville-Troike, M. 1982. *The Ethnography of Communication. An Introduction.* Oxford.

Scannel, P. 1991. *Broadcast Talk*. London.

Semino, E., J. Heywood, and M. Short. 2004. "Methodological Problems in the Analysis of Metaphors in a Corpus of Conversations about Cancer." *Journal of Pragmatics* 36:1271–1294.

Sontag, S. 1991. *Illness as Metaphor: AIDS and Its Metaphors*. London.

Tsitsanoudis-Mallidis, N. 2011. "The Transformation of Television Journalistic Discourse into an Object of Commercial Dealing. The Greek Case." *International Journal of Instructional Media* 38n2:133–146.

———. 2013. *Language and Greek Crisis: An Analysis of Form and Content*. New York.

———. 2014. "Interdisciplinary Approach of the Narrative Fairytale in Language Courses by Students of the Second Grade in a Greek Primary School." *International Research Journal for Quality in Education* 1n5:7–10.

Tsitsanoudis-Mallidis, N. and E. Derveni. 2018. "Emotive language: Linguistic Depictions of the Three-Year-Old Drowned Refugee Boy in the Greek Journalistic Discourse." *Interface: Journal of European Languages and Literatures* 6:1–38.

Tulloch, J. and A. Moran. 1986. *A Country Practice: Quality Soap*. Sydney.

Van Dijk, T. A. 1993. "Stories and Racism." In *Narrative and Social Control: Critical Perspectives*, ed. D.K. Mumby, 121–142. Newbury Park.

Van Leeuwen, T. 1996. "The Representation of Social Actors." In *Texts and Practices: Readings in Critical Discourse Analysis*, ed. C.R. Caldas–Coulthard and M. Coulthard. London.

Wittgenstein, L. 1989. *Philosophical Investigations*. Oxford. Orig. publ. in English in 1953. New York.

C. Web Links

The following electronic links are provided for further information. The numbers under each chapter correspond to the footnotes in which the links are mentioned.

Chapter 1

n7.   TED video titled "A Different Kind of Mistake" [Τὸ λάθος ἀλλιῶς]. Filmed March 11, 2018, in Thessaloniki. https://www.youtube.com/watch?v=c0t49NhrjYE

n10.   European Commission against Racism and Intolerance (ECRI) 2016 Annual Report. https://rm.coe.int/annual-report-on-ecri-s-activities-covering-the-period-from-1-january-/16808ae6d6

Article in *EFSYN*, "Φασιστική ρητορική η 'προστασία του ευρωπαϊκού τρόπου ζωής'" [Fascist rhetoric the "protection of the European way of life"], September 10, 2019. https://www.efsyn.gr/kosmos/eyropi/210239_fasistiki-ritoriki-i-prostasia-toy-eyropaikoy-tropoy-zois

n11.   Presentation on April 25 at the ERT Respect Words Seminar on journalistic language and hate speech held in Athens April 24-27, 2017, titled "Η Δημοσιογραφική γλώσσα ως όχημα αξιολογικών κρίσεων και διάδοσης/συντήρησης αρνητικών στερεότυπων" [Journalistic language as a vehicle for evaluative judgements and the spread/maintenance of negative stereotypes]. https://www.respectwords.org/el/seminar-ert/

Article in *To Vima*, Feb 6, 2019, titled "Η Σύρος και 'Η γλώσσα του άλλου'" [Syros and "the language of the other"]. https://www.tovima.gr/2019/02/06/culture/i-syros-kai-i-glossa-tou-allou/

Chapter 2

n3.   PDF of a paper presented by N. Tsitsanoudis-Mallidis, A. Lygoura, and D. Sakatzis at the Panhellenic Scientific Anniversary Conference, November 4, 2011, titled "Οι παρατηρούμενες αλλαγές στους συμβολισμούς της δημοτικής γλώσσας μετά το 1976" [The observed changes in the symbols of the demotic language after 1976]. http://ins.web.auth.gr/images/stories/Dion/%CE%A4%CE%A3%CE%99%CE%A4%CE%A3%CE%91%CE%9D%CE%9F%CE%A5%CE%94%CE%97%20%CE%BA.%CE%AC%201.pdf

Chapter 3

n3.   Discussion aired on ERT on December 7, 2013. YouTube video, 1:23:21. https://www.youtube.com/watch?v=j8W_AFJidmM>

n21. Article in *Ta Nea*, August 2, 2019. https://www.tanea.gr/2019/08/02/science-technology/i-texnologia-allazei-stadiaka-to-noima-ton-lekseon-pou-sxetizontai-me-ti-fysi/?fbclid=IwAR29nELDVNGvWq2OtjtwenY4ywN24KBUwS3NcdvpiFczAFX8-x1tmSvifsU>

n31. Summaries of my joint paper with E. Theodoropoulos and an additional paper I presented at the 3rd Panhellenic Conference of the Psychological Association of Northern Greece in Ioannina, October 9-11, 2015. https://psychology-lab.ecedu.uoi.gr/wp-content/uploads/2020/11/vivlio-perilipseon-3o-panellinio-synedrio-pseve-ptn.pdf

n32. Paper published December 2015 in the *Επιστημονική Επετηρίδα Παιδαγωγικού Τμήματος Νηπιαγωγών Πανεπιστημίου Ιωαννίνων* [Scientific yearbook of the pedagogy department of kindergarten teachers of the University of Ioannina], 5:150-181. https://www.researchgate.net/publication/304241641_Oi_glossikes_apeikoniseis_tes_oikonomikes_krises_ston_elleniko_diaphemistiko_logo_-_Endeiktikes_anaparastaseis_semerinon_nepion_kai_paidion

Chapter 4

n1. European Respect Words radio campaign. https://www.respectwords.org/el/%CE%B5%CE%BA%CF%83%CF%84%CF%81%CE%B1%CF%84%CE%B5%CE%B9%CE%B1/

n6. Official website of the International Summer University of the University of Ioannina on Greek Language, Culture, and Media. https://summerschool.ac.uoi.gr/

News articles about the International Summer University:

Koini Gnomi, "Ο πολιτισμός της Σύρου: Ο ορισμός της ποιότητας" [The culture of Syros: The definition of quality]. July 16, 2019. https://www.koinignomi.gr/news/politismos/2019/07/16/o-politismos-tis-syroy-o-orismos-tis-poiotitas.html?fbclid=IwAR1qbnbeWg0-V0-K0-FZqVHKvCk-dEj36y7l86UVvoK2aP548tX-l30ufen4

LIFO, "2o θερινό Πανεπιστήμιο: Ελληνική γλώσσα, πολιτισμός και μέσα μαζικής επικοινωνίας" [Second summer university: Greek language, culture and mass communication]. February 29, 2016. http://www.lifo. gr/market/marketnews/91662

Neos Kosmos, "Πρωτοποριακό το διεθνές θερινό πανεπιστήμιο 'Ελληνική γλώσσα, πολιτισμός και ΜΜΕ'" [The international summer university "Greek language, culture and media'" is a pioneer]. July 18, 2019. https://neoskosmos.com/el/221115/protoporiako-to-diethnes-therino-panepistimio-elliniki-glossa-politismos-kai-mme/?fbclid=IwAR1Q81FVAb3-aK7W-oppblq-zAA-oKDlgpgGnctLd2c-cr9OsmAtgMEVYMes

Real, "Η Ελλάδα σήμερα: Γλώσσα, Πολιτισμός και ΜΜΕ" [Greece today: Language, culture and media]. February 1, 2016. http://www.real.gr/ DefaultArthro.aspx?page=arthro&id=481559&catID=14

To Vima announcement regarding 2nd International Summer University. January 23, 2016. http://www.tovima.gr/culture/article/?aid=771206

To Vima, "Η Νικολέττα Τσιτσανούδη "Αυτοπροσώπως" στον Νίκο Θρασυβούλου" [Nikoletta Tsitsanidou "in person" to Niko Thrasivoulou.] May 20, 2016. http://www.tovima.gr/vimafm/article/?aid=801172

n9.   Article in *Avgi* titled "Η γλώσσα του 'άλλου'" [The language of the "other"]. May 17, 2019. https://www.avgi.gr/politiki/312150_i-glossa-toy-alloy?fbclid=IwAR0VH1OgYPq1Sdt2bhEowrImfjubvpFrMOD1GtznE1 8fuZ1fSFqWt5e3iOE n13

Index